MW00611032

SWANS, SWINE, AND SWINDLERS

HIGH RELIABILITY AND CRISIS MANAGEMENT

SERIES EDITORS Karlene H. Roberts and Ian I. Mitroff

SERIES TITLES

High Reliability Management: Operating on the Edge
By Emery Roe and Paul R. Schulman
2008

Dirty Rotten Strategies:
How We Trick Ourselves and Others into Solving the Wrong Problems
Precisely
By Ian I. Mitroff and Abraham Silvers
2010

SWANS, SWINE, AND SWINDLERS

Coping with the Growing Threat of Mega-Crises and Mega-Messes

Can M. Alpaslan
and Ian I. Mitroff

STANFORD BUSINESS BOOKS
An Imprint of Stanford University Press
Stanford, California

Stanford University Press
Stanford, California

Special discounts for bulk quantities of Stanford Business Books
are available to corporations, professional associations, and other
organizations. For details and discount information, contact the special
sales department of Stanford University Press.
Tel: (650) 736-1782, Fax: (650) 736-1784

Printed in the United States of America on acid-free, archival-quality paper

Library of Congress Cataloging-in-Publication Data

Alpaslan, Can M. (Can Murat), author.
  Swans, swine, and swindlers : coping with the growing threat of mega-crises
and mega-messes / Can M. Alpaslan and Ian I. Mitroff.
    pages cm. — (High reliability and crisis management)
  Includes bibliographical references and index.
  ISBN 978-0-8047-7137-5 (cloth : alk. paper)
    1. Crisis management. I. Mitroff, Ian I., author. II. Title. III. Series: High
reliability and crisis management.
  HD49.A47 2011
  658.4'77—dc22
                                              2011005045

Typeset by Bruce Lundquist in 10/15 Sabon

This book is dedicated to the memory of Russell Ackoff:
friend, mentor, and teacher.

In the book of life's questions, the answers are not in the back.

— CHARLES SCHULTZ

If everything is a mess, why not analyze and manage it that way?

— EMERY ROE

The common division of the world into subject and object, inner world and outer world, body and soul, is no longer adequate.

— WERNER HEISENBERG

CONTENTS

Testifying to the Financial Crisis Inquiry Commission, the body established by Congress to determine the causes of the Wall Street debacle, Lloyd C. Blankfein, the chairman and chief executive of Goldman Sachs, drew most of the fire.

Mr. Blankfein parried repeated questions over his bank's extraordinary profits and salaries. At one point, when he likened aspects of [the great financial crisis] to a "hurricane" and similar acts of God [that is, natural disasters], the commission's chairman, Phil Angelides, a Democrat and former California state treasurer, cut in to say, "Acts of God, we'll exempt. These were acts of men and women."

— SEWELL CHAN, *New York Times*, January 14, 2010

THE POTENTIAL IMPACT OF CRISES caused or exacerbated by humans is increasing exponentially. As the quote above suggests, the current financial crisis was not an act of God; it was an act of men and women. So are all crises. And there are at least three major human causes of crises.

Swans refers to false assumptions and mistaken beliefs in particular, and the inability to manage assumptions and beliefs in general, that can lead to crises. We derive the term from the book *The Black Swan: The Impact of the Highly Improbable*, by Nassim Nicholas Taleb. Black swans are highly improbable events that have extremely large impacts.[1] What turns a black swan event into a crisis is mismanagement.[2] For instance, the current financial crisis happened partly because Wall Street has fostered a culture that systematically ignored black swan events. Note that the current financial crisis was not a black swan event.[3] Financial crises have been with us for a very long time and happen almost on a regular basis.[4]

Swine refers to greed, hubris, or arrogance, and the inability to design and operate systems that can minimize those traits. If drilling the deepest oil and gas well ever in history reflects BP and Transocean's "intensive planning and focus on effective operations," as the Transocean CEO had said,[5] then causing and failing to contain one of the largest oil spills in history shows much more than negligence, foolishness, or a lack of crisis management capacity. It shows the greedy, arrogant, and even narcissistic side of these organizations. It also shows that these types of organizations are not designed and monitored effectively, sanctioned, or punished such that they are deterred from engaging in behaviors that put the rest of us and nature at risk.

Swindlers refers to unethical and corrupt behaviors, and of course, the inability to monitor, detect, and stop such behaviors. Bernie Madoff's Ponzi scheme, Enron's collapse, and Worldcom's bankruptcy are just a few examples. The types of crises caused by swindlers send out a trail of early warning signals long before they occur. But for various reasons, such as confused organizational priorities, and individuals' and organizations' inability to pick up signals or connect the dots, these crises are often not prevented before they happen.

Of course, these three types of causes are interrelated and not mutually exclusive. Downplaying the significance of black swan events may be due to arrogance, over-confidence bias, or situational factors such as a dysfunctional reward-incentive system, whereas intentionally failing to prepare for black swan events can be due to low or nonexistent ethical standards. Cutting back on safety without violating regulations may be due to greed, arrogance, habit, cost-cutting pressures, normalization of deviance, or a lack of understanding of the complexities of a system. Violating regulations intentionally because paying off fines is cheaper than adhering to regulations can be due to low ethical standards as well as ineffective regulations and intense competition.

While, as noted, the potential impact of crises is increasing exponentially, our ability to prevent or respond to crises properly seems to increase only linearly at best. A proper response to a crisis requires at a minimum a more comprehensive set of critical thinking skills, a higher level of emotional intelligence, and a higher level of moral development. Our goal in this book is to provide a set of tools, concepts, frameworks, and perspectives that the reader can use to understand crises better and manage them more properly.

CENTRAL CONCEPTS: CRISES AND MESSES

Two critical concepts—crises and messes—play central roles throughout this book. As a result, both concepts are not only used constantly but continually refined and redefined as we proceed. Nonetheless, precisely because they are so central and critical, we need to give some preliminary definitions and understandings of both terms.

Russell Ackoff was the first to appropriate the expression *mess* to stand for a system of problems that are so interrelated that they cannot be separated in principle, in practice, or, most fundamental of all, in their basic existence:

[People] are not confronted with problems that are independent of each other, but with dynamic situations that consist of complex systems of changing problems that interact with each other. . . . I call such situations *messes*. Problems are abstractions extracted from messes by analysis.[6]

Therefore, when a mess, which is a system of problems, is taken apart, [i.e., analyzed] it loses its essential properties and so does each of its parts. The behavior of a mess depends more on how the treatment of its parts interact than how they act independently of each other. *A partial solution to a whole system of problems is better than whole solutions of each of its parts taken separately* [emphasis added].[7]

In other words, none of the problems that are parts of a mess can be taken apart and analyzed independently of all the other problems that constitute the mess. In slightly different words, a mess is a *complex system* of problems that are so tightly bound together that the problems are not only inseparable, they don't even exist apart from the system of which they are a part. For instance, the "education problem," or better yet the "education mess," doesn't exist apart from other messes such as crime, health care, poverty, real estate values, and so on. In this way, the concept of a "mess" is essentially synonymous with the concept of a "system."

If we substitute the term *crisis* for *problem* in the preceding definition of a mess, then as we show later, every crisis is part of a larger mess. In fact, there is no such thing as a single crisis that is not embedded in a system of other crises. Thus, while crises and messes are often taken to be the same, they are not. The most important difference is, while all crises are messes, not all messes are necessarily crises.

The reverse also holds true: if a supposed crisis can be addressed or resolved completely independently of other crises, then it is not a crisis. Moreover, the common notion that a crisis can be addressed or resolved independently of other crises (for example, the belief that the current financial crisis can be addressed only by financial remedies completely independently of all the other crises that contributed to it or those that the financial crisis contributed to) is a surefire recipe for a bigger crisis or mess.

MEGA-CRISES AND MEGA-MESSES

Given the preceding, the "Great Financial Crisis of 2008–9" is by any measure a *mega-crisis*. It will make it harder to cope with a set of already existing crises such as the drug-trafficking crisis in Central America, homeland security, inner-city crime, and so on. It may also set off new crises such as currency wars or even actual wars, as the history of financial crises had demonstrated. In fact, if the prognosticators are right, and if this crisis is anything like what Japan went through in the 1990s, it could be decades before it's over.

If this weren't bad enough, the financial crisis is also a *mega-mess*; that is, it is a whole system of interdependent messes that must be addressed simultaneously.[8] For instance, the mess that is Wall Street is not independent of the health care mess or the social security mess or the global warming mess. There is little doubt that the huge deficits that the United States is incurring to bail itself out of the current fiasco will be felt for years. Furthermore, unless they are managed very carefully, the actions the U.S. government takes in responding to today's mega-mess could well lead to even worse crises in the future.

A mega-mess is a bigger mess. But the difference between the two is not only something out there in the world, something that exists independently of all observing minds, or something that all observing minds agree on. There is no agreed-upon scale or scope, and often the absence of scale and scope becomes a big part of the mess. This is the point of Chapter 7, that, at different levels of awareness, these definitions differ drastically. In all seriousness, sometimes, "clear" definitions are what get us into a mess. Think about a clear definition of *fetus* in the context of abortion, how such definitions differ on both sides of the aisle. Also consider the following: a crisis cannot be managed independently of other crises. Doing so may create mega-crises by intensifying a number of other crises and create new ones. All crises are messes, and a mess is a system of problems. A mega-mess is a bigger mess; it is a system of messes. A mega-mess may refer to a crisis because all crises are messes.

At the time of this writing, national and international public health organizations have responded to the H1N1 swine flu epidemic. In retrospect, it was not the crisis it was presumed to be. Nonetheless, if it had been a true epidemic—indeed if it had become a pandemic— then it could have further hampered economic recovery. If people were afraid to leave their homes and venture out in public, then this could have seriously depressed consumer traffic in shopping malls, attendance at sporting events, and so on. After all, the economic cost of the 2003 SARS crisis was estimated to be around $11–18 billion and the economic output losses in Asian countries around 0.5–2 percent.[9]

The point is that in today's world, it is not enough, if it ever was, to prepare for individual crises in isolation. One must plan and prepare for the simultaneous occurrence of multiple crises or catastrophes. One also needs to consider how the effects of multiple crises can reinforce one another so that the overall result is worse than if merely one occurred by itself. The fact that this process is complex, uncertain, and never perfect is not an excuse for doing nothing. How one can most effectively manage mega-crises and mega-messes is the subject of this book.

All Crises Are Human-Caused

While it has become commonplace to say that the current financial crisis is the biggest economic crisis we have faced since the Great Depression, it is far less of a truism to suggest that it is also one of the largest man-made or *human-caused* crises that we have ever experienced. Indeed, recall the statements of Lloyd C. Blankfein, the chairman of Goldman Sachs, to the Financial Crisis Inquiry Commission in the epigraph to the Preface. Contrary to Mr. Blankfein's contentions, the financial crisis is not a natural disaster over which we have no control and, therefore, "like earthquakes and tsunamis *just happen* from time-to-time." In fact, as we shall see, *all crises* are human-caused. (As of this writing, the world has responded, however imperfectly, to a horrendous earthquake in Haiti. As we explain later, the earthquake is without any doubt a serious natural hazard, but the crisis is human-caused. Humans are responsible for the substandard and shoddy construction that collapsed in the quake, not Mother Nature.)

Consider the following: If the financial system works well and, in fact, if it works too well in the sense that it's less volatile and more predictable, then people are encouraged to take more risks.[10] This stands in sharp contrast to *the ideal* of other systems, such as the airline industry, in which accidents and mishaps are a mandate to take even fewer risks and to keep reducing the accident rate. To repeat, if the financial system is stable and it tolerates a certain level of risk taking, then people take even greater risks, which eventually leads to a crisis.[11] Indeed, as we show later, the culture of the finance industry is such that it virtually guarantees the production of major crises on a regular basis.[12]

Follow the chain further: the more that the finance sector invents financial instruments to spread individual risk by combining them into shared packages, the more that the financial system tolerates risk. As a result, banks lend or borrow more money relative to the funds that they keep in reserve to pay off debts. But in this way, the spreading of individual risk also increases systemic risk.[13] Since neither leveraging nor the spreading of risk is sustainable, when a crisis eventually happens, it is even worse than if it occurred sooner. The point is that every step is due to the collective actions of people, not impersonal forces of nature.

Perhaps John Cassidy of the *New Yorker* said it best: "The real causes of the [financial] crisis are much scarier and less amenable to reform: they have to do with the inner logic of an economy like ours. *The root problem is what might be termed 'rational irrationality'—behavior that, on the individual level, is perfectly reasonable but that, when aggregated in* [a complex *system*], *produces calamity*"[emphasis added].[14]

General Lessons, General Patterns

As big as the current financial crisis is, it is not the only huge crisis that we can expect in our lifetimes. In fact, new crises are constantly brewing, some of which are due to the current financial crisis. Therefore it is absolutely imperative that we learn—as quickly as possible—the lessons that the crises we have experienced have to teach us. It is even more imperative that we put those lessons into practice.

For the purposes of this book, we need to examine a broad range of crises. Only in this way can we see both the general and the precise patterns that virtually all crises follow. Furthermore, although they are certainly not identical by any means, essentially all crises obey the same patterns. This only makes the following questions more critical: "Why have we been so unable and unwilling to learn from past mega-crises?" and "What are the prospects for our doing a better job of anticipating and preparing for future mega-crises?"

Crises Involve Every Known Field of Inquiry

There is another daunting fact about modern crises. Due to their messy, that is, complex, nature, they involve every known field of inquiry and profession in their definition and treatment. This is precisely why crises and messes are so difficult to understand and manage. Their "definition," let alone "solution," cannot be found in any single field of inquiry or profession. No field or profession has a monopoly on dealing with them. In more pithy terms, no field or profession "completely owns" a crisis or a mess.

As a result, every crisis calls for interdisciplinary, and even transdisciplinary, thinking. They also call for intense cooperation and deep integration across the widest possible array of professions. It only stands to reason that if crises are the result of a system of problems that are highly interactive, then their solutions, if they exist, can only be created by a system of disciplines and professions that are highly interactive as well. Unfortunately, this rarely occurs.[15]

Consider the environmental aspects of the financial crisis. There are not only the obvious environmental components such as how to create new green jobs and industries that will hopefully get us out of the crisis by decreasing our unhealthy dependency on foreign oil, but also slightly less visible environmental dimensions as well. If people have less income, let alone no job, then cities and states stand to receive significantly less in tax revenues; therefore, cities and states are less able to maintain public parks and green areas and, in many cases, to prevent or contain wildfires. They are also less able to enforce environmental standards and regulations. Contributions to environmental organizations also decrease, further affecting the deterioration of the environment.

Consider public health and safety. It is well known that when people lose their jobs, then incidences of crime, such as child abuse and spousal abuse, go up in number, thereby constituting a potential public health and welfare crisis. In addition, people put off going to their doctors, so the chances of epidemics increase. If another crisis such as swine flu also occurs simultaneously, then because of the economic downturn, there is potentially less money available to treat it. But if people are afraid to leave their houses because of the flu, then this can have the extra effect of further decreasing economic activity. In this way, if not managed properly, every crisis has the potential to spread.

There are many more perspectives than environmental, public health, and public safety that one needs to consider in order to understand the causes and consequences of the financial crisis. In the following chapters, we give a more detailed, comprehensive, and transdisciplinary explanation of this and other crises.

Crises and Messes Are Not Like Exercises

As Charles Schultz reminds us, crises and messes are not like the nice neat tidy exercises that are found at the ends of the overwhelming majority of textbooks. Textbooks constitute the bulk of K–12 and even college undergraduate education, so most people are primed to expect exercises even when they are not appropriate. Because many people experience extreme discomfort when they first encounter real problems, far too many "crisis exercises" end up being overly structured and predictable, even though they are supposed to be open-ended and, therefore, more like problems.

Unlike real problems, exercises have one and only one solution at which everyone is expected to arrive. Even more fundamental, exercises have only one definition or formulation. It is, in fact, precisely the single definition that is "given" to students in the typical, so-called "statement of the 'problem.'" Indeed, the phrase "the statement of the 'problem'" is a misnomer because a more correct statement is "the statement of the 'exercise.'" Furthermore, once solved, exercises remain solved forever. This is not so with real problems.

Real problems have none of the characteristics of exercises. If anything is symptomatic of crises and messes, it is the fact that they are unbounded. They resist our attempts to confine them and rein them in by reducing them to a single discipline or point of view. For example, different stakeholders rarely have the same definition of the individual problems that constitute a mess and of the entire mess itself. Indeed, the fact that different stakeholders have different perceptions of a mess is itself one of the key defining attributes of messes! As a result, "problem negotiation" is one of the most important aspects of managing messes. Before one can "solve" a problem one first has to agree on the "nature" of the problem. And if agreement is arrived at all, it should be reached only at the end of an *intense* debate about the "nature" of the problem instead of the all-too-common pressure to get a quick consensus.

Every Crisis Is a Crisis of Meaning

Virtually every crisis has a religious or spiritual component. Consider the religious and spiritual aspects of the current financial crisis.

Crises as great and as profound as the financial crisis constitute a severe threat to our psychological health and well-being. They do this by threatening our basic assumptions about the goodness, predictability, and stability of our fellow beings and the world itself. Great catastrophes and crises test our fundamental philosophical, religious, and spiritual beliefs and principles to the very core of our being. In short, they test our mettle in ways like nothing else. For example, people may become more religious and spiritual; fundamentalists, on the other hand, may try to blame others for causing the crisis.

There are also less obvious consequences. Crises bring out aspects of religion that are normally hidden from view. For instance, the *San Francisco Chronicle* reported that Islamic funds have suffered less during the current economic crisis:

Renouncing interest is the high-profile element of Islamic finance that relates to the current economic crisis. For Islamically [*sic*] correct investors, that means there are limits to how much debt that a company can have or how much profit it can derive from interest-based payments. That criterion eliminated the possibility of holding stocks in financial services companies, like Citigroup or Washington Mutual, whose stocks lost 86 percent of all their value last year, respectively.

Islamic finance also prohibits selling assets you don't own, selling someone's debt and engaging in high-risk investments. Thus, there was no participation in practices that have been blamed for Wall Street's meltdown: complex derivatives trading, short-selling and the $30 trillion market in credit default swaps.[16]

This is not to say that Islamic funds are without problems. For instance, they often underperform the S&P 500. Nonetheless, the point is that one doesn't have to dig deep and far to show that crises involve every known field of human inquiry and profession. Once again, they involve every aspect of our lives—especially those that we consider to be the most personal and private such as religion and spirituality, and that seemingly have the least to do with the crises at hand.

The Moral

The moral is, unless one learns how to understand, treat, and manage crises as messes, then one cannot understand, treat, and manage crises at all. The trouble is that the vast majority of crises are never understood, treated, and managed as messes. The result is that most crises are managed poorly. The consequence is an even bigger crisis and mess than the original one.

THE AIM OF THIS BOOK

The aim of this book is to help the reader deal better with mega-crises through a better understanding of how and why mega-crises are mega-messes. To achieve this aim, the chapters are focused on the key elements of crises and messes, and especially the key lessons they have to teach.

The book is organized into three parts. Part I is concerned with uncovering or surfacing the key underlying assumptions that often lead to crises and that with almost no exceptions all crises undermine and invalidate. Each of the five chapters in Part I identifies a different type and body of assumptions.

A major crisis does not merely challenge or upset our key operating assumptions. It does something far worse. It "destroys" all or nearly all of the key assumptions we make about ourselves, others, our organizations and institutions, and the world in general. By invalidating and destroying our key beliefs, a crisis literally pulls the proverbial rug out from under us. Because different crises invalidate different types of assumptions, we have to explore as many different types of crises and assumptions as we can in order to reduce the number of missed assumptions to as few as possible.

If Part I is concerned with identifying as many key assumptions as possible, then Part II is concerned with how we can better manage assumptions and, thereby, crises and messes. Specifically, Chapter 6 discusses a set of strategies to overcome the emotional difficulties of managing assumptions, crises, and messes; Chapter 7 outlines a set of philosophical frameworks to overcome the cognitive difficulties of doing so. Part III applies to the financial sector some of the central concepts discussed in the book. Whereas Chapter 8 outlines an inquiry methodology one can use to make sense of the financial crisis, Chapter 9 examines in greater detail the role of mistaken beliefs, false assumptions, and trust in financial systems. It also suggests four essential trust-enhancing elements for a high reliability financial sector.

This book is concerned with assumptions because assumptions, not facts, are the fundamental building blocks of reality. Assumptions are basic because there is no way that we can ever know with complete certainty everything we need and would like to know about the world. We have no choice but to make assumptions if we are to function.

Ordinarily, we have no need to examine and to challenge our everyday assumptions. But preparing for crises is another matter. Effective crisis preparation demands that we know and debate the key assumptions upon which all our crisis plans and procedures rest.

While this book draws heavily from the traditional academic literature on crises, it also ventures far beyond it. It considers ideas that are not contained in the typical treatments of catastrophes, disasters, crises, and so on. The fundamental reason is that the topic of messes necessitates it. For this reason, we use ideas from fields as diverse and varied as human development, philosophy, the psychoanalysis of organizations, and organizational health.

We would be remiss if we failed to note that, at best, the concept of messes has only been touched on in passing in previous books on crisis management.[17] The idea of mega-messes has not been broached at all, let alone received the systematic attention it deserves.

For the most part, the academic research on crisis management has focused mainly on the study of a few isolated variables.[18] As a result, previous research has not focused on one of the key characteristics of mega-crises, the fact that they are parts of complex and messy systems. By not recognizing and treating both the systemic and messy nature of crises, the danger is that we make crises worse.

SWANS, SWINE,
AND SWINDLERS

PART I

UNCOVERING
ASSUMPTIONS

I

A CRISIS IS NOT
WHAT WE HAVE BEEN
LED TO BELIEVE
Every Crisis Is an Existential Crisis of Meaning

There is a central human experience that will shake us to the roots and that each of us must eventually face. Nobody likes to acknowledge or talk much about it. So we usually try to ignore it, wrapping ourselves in habitual routines to avoid having to face it. Since there is no ready-made term for this experience, I will call it *the moment of world collapse.* . . .

World collapse occurs when the props that have supported our life give way unexpectedly. Suddenly the meaning our life previously had seems to lack weight and substance and no longer nourishes us as it did before.

—JOHN WELWOOD, *Toward a Psychology of Awakening*

IN COMMON PARLANCE, a crisis is an unexpected event that causes, or has the potential to cause, severe loss of lives, serious injuries, and widespread destruction of property, and to exact serious financial costs. In addition, something is usually considered to be a major crisis *if and only if* it attracts serious media attention. Further, a major crisis also has the potential to destroy an individual or an organization, or to bring a major institution to its knees.

While the preceding definition applies to every crisis of which the authors are aware, it does not capture fully what a crisis does to those it affects. In this sense, while true, the definition is incomplete. In fact, the commonly held belief that there must be a single, universal definition of a crisis is wrong. If there were universal agreement on the definition and meaning of crises or "messes," then they would not be "messes." Instead, the varying meanings and definitions of crises provide valuable information about the assumptions that people make about crises and their prevention and containment.[1]

If there is a common property that all crises share it is the fact that *every* crisis destroys the underlying assumptions ("props") we have been making about ourselves, the goodness and the safety of our society, and the world in general. This is precisely why crises are so traumatic. In one fell swoop, they turn our lives completely upside down. They not only disturb but seriously threaten our very existence by undermining the bedrock assumptions that we use to give meaning, purpose, and a sense of stability to our lives. As a result, we feel deeply abandoned and betrayed. This is why every crisis is a deep existential crisis of meaning. In short, every crisis is a *moment of world collapse.*

A DEADLY EXAMPLE: OKLAHOMA CITY

On April 19, 1995, the Alfred P. Murrah Federal Office Building in downtown Oklahoma City was bombed. The result was that 168 people were killed, 19 of whom were children, and over 800 were injured. It was the deadliest act of terrorism on U.S. soil prior to the attacks of 9/11.

As horrific as the tragic loss of lives was, it became clear to the authors through analysis of countless hours of televised coverage plus many written accounts of the tragedy that the true definition and meaning of the crisis was rooted in something deeper and thus much less apparent. The bombing not only blew up a building and took countless lives, it ripped a set of basic, fundamental, taken-for-granted, largely unconscious assumptions out from under the citizens of Oklahoma City in particular and the United States in general. In other words, it was a true moment of world collapse. As a result, Oklahoma City revealed the existential dimensions of crises and tragedies and a whole different definition of them, which had been virtually ignored and unfortunately still is.

To see this, consider again the typical definition of a crisis.[2] A crisis is a sudden, unexpected event that has the potential to

1. cause serious injuries or diseases, and raise public health concerns and issues;

2. lead to deaths;

3. exact major financial costs;

4. destroy an individual or organization;

5. cause serious damage to a whole society;

6. attract serious media attention.

There is little doubt that Oklahoma City satisfied almost all of the components of the preceding definition. Notice carefully that a "potential crisis" does not have to satisfy all of the components in order to qualify as a "crisis." For this very reason, the determination of what is a crisis is not an exercise in applying a static definition. Instead, it is part of an ongoing process or mess.

Thus, while the preceding definition applies, it became clear that something else was operating. Again, through our extensive media analysis, it became clear to us that prior to the tragedy, the citizens of Oklahoma City and the rest of the United States held at least three major assumptions as to why such an act would *not* take place on U.S. soil and, furthermore, would *not* be perpetrated by a U.S. citizen:

1. Terrorism does not happen in America, and certainly not in the heartland of America; terrorism only happens in Europe, the Middle East, and other dangerous regions of the world.

2. Americans are not terrorists, period! Therefore, an American would never commit an act of terrorism against fellow Americans, and certainly not on American soil.

3. Innocent men, women, and especially children will not be killed to "further the cause" of terrorists.

In other words, the tragedy was not only completely unexpected, it made no sense at all because it was completely unthinkable.

It is especially important to note that a major crisis does not merely destroy one or two of our basic assumptions. It simultaneously destroys *all or nearly all* of our important beliefs. Most of us can manage if one or two of our assumptions are destroyed, but we have a much harder time if a large chunk of our foundation is destroyed suddenly and at once.[3]

9/11 WENT EVEN FURTHER

Consider the assumptions that were destroyed by 9/11:[4]

1. The two oceans are a "protective moat" that can shield the United States from foreign terrorists; that is, foreign terrorists cannot and will not attack us on our home shores.

2. The U.S. government agencies that are supposed to defend us from attack can be depended upon to do their jobs and hence intercept terrorists before they can attack us; that is, they are competent, flexible, and innovative; they willingly share information among themselves; they integrate the information in a timely manner and get it to the right persons; and so on. For instance, the appropriate agencies will be proactive enough to pay attention to those who are attending flight schools and are learning merely how to take off planes but not to land them. In short, foreign terrorists cannot slip through the defenses of the United States.

3. Two of the central symbols of capitalism (the Twin Towers and Wall Street) and the symbol of national defense (the Pentagon) will not and cannot be completely destroyed and certainly not attacked simultaneously.

One could, of course, add other assumptions as well. But the point should be clear. Every crisis raises to the surface a set of background assumptions that we have been making, mostly unconsciously. And then, seemingly without warning, it quickly destroys those presumptions.[5]

A MORE GENERAL SET OF ASSUMPTIONS

As a result of the foregoing, it is not hard to see that every major crisis challenges and destroys a more general set of assumptions:

1. We are exempt from a particular set of crises by virtue of our location, a special set of circumstances, our industry and types of products, and so on. This is the "exemption clause" or belief; it is also the belief of why we, as a people, are special. The myth of exceptionalism is deeply enshrined in American history.[6]

2. Things will continue to behave as they always have; in other words, there is almost always a "continuity" assumption of some sort that expresses the belief that things will continue as they always have. For instance, we are fundamentally safe and secure and we will continue to be so. The future will be like the past. A common expression is, "Our business, industry, and products have never been attacked in the past; therefore, there is no reason to believe that they will be in the future."

3. Certain things will probably never happen; this is similar to the "continuity" assumption in the sense that "discontinuities" are extremely rare events, or, in other words, they are "black swans." As a result, we behave and think like Bertrand Russell's "inductivist turkeys" that never realize that because they have not had their heads cut off for five hundred days in a row is no guarantee that they will never have their heads cut off.

4. We can trust people in general not to betray and to harm us. We can trust those in charge (the government, company executives, and so on) to do their duty to protect us. These are basic trust assumptions.

5. We can trust our organizations and institutions to function well. For instance, my company, and indeed, my entire industry (for example, the financial sector), can be counted on implicitly to be and to do "good," that is, "do the right things."

6. We can trust technology to protect us; in other words, technology works for us on our behalf. Like item 4, items 5 and 6 are different kinds of trust assumptions.

7. People in general share the same values and therefore will act, or not act, as we do; in short, not only can we trust our neighbors, we can depend on them because they are like us. This is obviously a similarity assumption.

A SENSE OF MORAL OUTRAGE

Unfortunately, crises do more than merely shatter our fundamental assumptions and hurl us into an existential funk. They trigger a long list of intense emotional responses and thereby produce a deep sense of moral outrage.

Consider the insurance giant AIG. It is certainly true that in terms of the billions of dollars given to AIG in order to bail it out, the millions of dollars in bonuses for the very executives that initially got us into the mess represents a tiny amount, approximately one-tenth of a percent. But this misses the whole point. Compared to the billions, the bonuses may only be a small amount, but compared to what the average person earns in his or her entire lifetime, they are huge. And they loom even larger given the millions who are out of work and have no paychecks at all.

To assume that people will respond calmly, coolly, and rationally to major crises would be laughable if it were not so far off the mark and if it didn't add insult to injury. The fact that humans do not respond coolly and unemotionally is exceedingly important. It constitutes one of the biggest reasons why the economic profession as a whole failed to sense the current financial crisis: *the basic models and modes of thinking that economists use are seriously deficient because they do not incorporate the fact that humans are governed by deep feelings and emotions.*[7] In fact, most economists either assume feelings and emotions away or focus on a tiny few. For instance, in *Emotions in Finance*,[8] Jocelyn Pixley demonstrates that the field of finance has built its theories upon a base of four and only four emotions: fear, greed, trust, and uncertainty.

To anyone who knows even the very least about emotional intelligence, this is not only absurd but completely outrageous. First, there are obviously many more emotions than four (for instance, grief, happiness, joy, remorse, sadness, shame, pride, and so on). Indeed, the first mark of emotional intelligence is the sheer number of emotions that one can name and identify. To name only four emotions is itself a major sign of low emotional intelligence. Second, as a result, one of the least acknowledged reasons responsible for the current financial mess is the fact that the economics and finance professions have built theories that are impoverished emotionally. For instance, in transaction cost economics and agency theory (two of the major theories that are pursued by academics in business schools), individuals are assumed to pursue their own self-interest with guile, as well as deception, coercion, and fraudulent behavior.[9] Economics and finance may delude themselves that one can build theories upon such meager bases, but given the intense emotions that crises unleash, we can't build theories of crisis management upon such impoverished foundations.

A STRONG IMPLICATION

A strong implication follows immediately from the preceding. While the dictionary distinguishes between so-called natural disasters, catastrophes, and man-made or human-caused crises—as an indication that society generally takes this distinction for granted—we cannot. There is nothing "natural" about disasters that are caused or exacerbated by humans.

Professor Robert Bea of the Department of Civil and Environmental Engineering at the University of California, Berkeley, puts it bluntly. Bea makes a fundamental distinction between "natural *hazards*" and "human-caused *crises*."[10] For instance, no one doubts that an earthquake is a natural hazard. But if we build shoddy houses and buildings that crumble at the first tremors of an earthquake, and (among many other factors) our institutions are not designed to enforce regulations properly, then we become more vulnerable to a natural hazard and turn it into a human-caused crisis (Haiti is unfortunately the latest tragic example). While we certainly can't prevent all natural hazards from occurring, we can, through better knowledge and proper mitigation, prevent many if not most crises from happening.

In this sense, we regard *all* disasters, catastrophes, and crises as human-caused. To repeat, *every crisis is the result of the collapse or failure of a set of important assumptions that a set of stakeholders has made about why a certain set of disasters, catastrophes, and crises will or will not happen.* (For example, in the case of a building, a prime assumption is that it has been properly designed, built, maintained, and inspected.) More often than not, our assumptions "explain" why our special location, set of presumed safeguards, crisis plans and procedures, and so on will shield us from a set of disasters, catastrophes, and crises. But the primary point is that it is humans that have assumptions. Indeed, everything that humans do rests upon sets of stated and unstated, examined and unexamined assumptions. Most of the time, if we had to state and examine our assumptions, we'd literally be driven mad. Thus it behooves most of us to go about our daily lives by not examining our assumptions. The same cannot be said of those who need to practice crisis management effectively. We do not have the luxury of being unaware about our fundamental beliefs.

A GENERAL FRAMEWORK

Let us summarize the discussion thus far by presenting a general framework that we will use throughout this book both to organize and to make sense of the various concepts and topics we shall present. The basic framework is shown in Figure 1.1.

The framework derives from the work of Isabel Briggs Myers and her mother, which in turn is based on the work of Carl Jung.[11] It consists of two basic dimensions: the horizontal, which pertains to the *scope* or the *size* of a problem or situation that a person is inherently (instinctually) comfortable in dealing with, and the vertical, which pertains to the kind of *decision-making process* that a person inherently (instinctually) brings to bear on a problem or situation.[12] With regard to the first dimension, one either breaks a

Analytical or Technical

	1 Details, facts, formulas, here and now	2 The big picture, multiple interpretations, systems, future possibilities	
Parts	4 Specific individuals, stories, personal values, feelings	3 Communities and the entire planet, governance, societal values, politics	Whole

Personal or People

FIGURE 1.1.   The general framework

complex problem down into tiny, separate "parts" or "individual people" or looks at the larger, whole system or human community. With regard to the second dimension, one brings either an impersonal, analytical, cognitive process or an intensely personal, human process to bear in order to make an important decision. Combining the ends of both dimensions results in the four basic psychological or social orientations shown in Figure 1.1. Indeed, Figures 1.2 and

Analytical or Technical

	1 Severity of injuries, number of deaths, financial costs, collapse of companies	2 Interdependency of crises triggered, systemic costs, collapse of systems and industries	
Parts	4 Tragic stories of lost or hurt individuals, emotional costs, collapse of personal assumptions	3 Tragic stories of hurt communities, societal costs, collapse of societal assumptions	Whole

Personal or People

FIGURE 1.2.   The different definitions of crises

Analytical or Technical

1 Our technology is reliable and it will protect us.	2 Our systems are reliable and will protect us.
4 My immediate work group, family, and I are good, and will not betray or harm anyone.	3 My country, community, company, and industry are good and will not betray or harm us.

Parts   Whole

Personal or People

FIGURE 1.3.   Differing assumptions

1.3 show how the framework can be used to understand how the different definitions of crises and the different kinds of assumptions arise. The definitions and assumptions are the result of underlying attitudes or stances with regard to the world. Needless to say, as we proceed, we will make constant reference to the framework and explain and explore it further.

Finally, the framework is important because it shows how and why on any issue or problem of importance there are at least four very different attitudes or stances with regard to the issue or problem. But the framework is also important because underlying it is the fundamental philosophical and psychological assumption that none of the four cells or positions is more important or more basic than any of the others. Indeed, each position or stance picks up a basic sense or meaning of an important issue or problem that the others either ignore or dismiss altogether. As a result, the framework proves exceedingly valuable in helping us to identify our fundamental assumptions and beliefs as well as to define and to treat mega-messes and mega-crises.

CONCLUDING REMARKS

The collapse of assumptions is certainly not the only prominent feature that defines major crises. But it is without a doubt one of the most important. In the following chapters, we not only will examine other prominent features of crises but also will see how they reveal other major assumptions that crises destroy. For instance, in the case of the current financial crisis, other key assumptions have to do with whether one can trust a particular finance company and the entire finance industry not to betray the average investor as well as those who work in the industry. An important assumption is, not only am I good, but my company and industry are as well.

We will unearth other assumptions by zeroing in on the "unthinkables," the unstated and unexamined beliefs that prior to a crisis are believed will be true forever and hence can never be destroyed. Examining the broadest possible set of "unthinkables" is, in fact, the key to managing mega-crises and mega-messes.

Our ultimate goal is to help the reader identify more quickly, accurately, and effectively as many of the critical assumptions as possible upon which the actions one takes in a crisis depend and upon which the plans one formulates in advance for dealing with crises depend as well.

But before we can do this, we need to turn to an understanding of mega-messes.

WHAT IS A MESS?

The Fundamental Differences Between

Exercises, Problems, and Messes

The notion that your beloved pet could escape the yard and be put to death before you even have time to post flyers is a real possibility because of California's budget crisis.

—PETER FIMRITE, *San Francisco Chronicle*, September 8, 2009

After the mortgage business imploded last year, Wall Street investment banks began searching for another big idea to make money. They think they have found one. The bankers plan to buy "life settlements," life insurance policies that ill and elderly people sell for cash—$400,000 for a $1 million policy, say, depending on the life expectancy of the insured person. Then they plan to "securitize" these policies, in Wall Street's jargon, by packaging hundreds or thousands together into bonds. They will then resell those bonds to investors, like big pension funds, who will receive the payouts when people with the insurance die.

—JENNY ANDERSON, *New York Times*, September 6, 2009

A MESS IS THE WORLD'S WAY of telling us that we have been defining our problems too narrowly. Essentially, the world is telling us that reality is too complex to be captured within the narrow confines of how we normally think, how we have been traditionally educated, and how we normally work.

This chapter starts with Russell Ackoff's initial definition of a mess as a system of dynamically changing and interacting problems. But it ends with a very different and expanded definition.

The moral of the chapter is, expand every system of problems (mess) right up to and as far beyond your comfort zone as you, your organization, and society can tolerate. This is not only a moral imperative, it is also the only insurance we have against the cardinal sins of defining important problems too narrowly and solving the wrong problems precisely.

ACKOFF'S DEFINITION OF A MESS

Because it is the major idea behind this chapter, we want to repeat the quote from the Preface in which Russell Ackoff defined a mess. We want to start with Ackoff for two reasons: one, because to our knowledge, he was the first to define a mess, and, two, we need to go beyond his initial definition.

[People] are not confronted with problems that are independent of each other, but with dynamic situations that consist of complex systems of changing problems that interact with each other. . . . I call such situations *messes*. Problems are abstractions extracted from messes by analysis. . . . [1]

Therefore, when a mess, which is a system of problems, is taken apart [i.e., analyzed], it loses its essential properties and so does each of its parts. The behavior of a mess depends more on how the treatment of its parts interact than how they act independently of each other. *A partial solution to a whole system of problems is better than whole solutions of each of its parts taken separately* [emphasis added].[2]

Because the concept of a mess is defined in terms of the concept of a problem, we therefore need to say something about problems. Furthermore, because problems are often confused with exercises, we also need to delineate the differences between the two. The distinction between exercises, problems, and messes is important for the following reason. Trying to solve a problem independent of other problems is at least one level removed from reality. In the case of exercises, the situation is even worse. One is two levels removed.

EXERCISES VERSUS PROBLEMS

Unfortunately, from grammar school through college—and beyond— we are not generally taught the differences between exercises and problems. Over and over again, the impression is conveyed that they are the same when they are not.[3]

For instance, "If Billy has saved $6 and he needs $11 to buy a game, how much more money does he need to save?" is a simple *word exercise*. It is not a problem. For this reason, calling it a "word problem" is not only fundamentally misleading, it is plain wrong.

First, the exercise about Billy is already preformulated so that the student does not have to undertake the difficult task of determining what the problem is in the first place. What are the boundaries of the problem? What are the context and the environment within which it exists? What are the variables drawn from which discipline(s) that will be used to frame the problem? Whom does the problem affect? How serious is it for whom? In other words, So what? What's riding on the solution? Who cares?

If we were asked to find all of the legitimate ways in which Billy could raise the extra amount of money that he needs to buy a game, and the particular ways that were applicable to his life situation, then we would have a true problem, not an exercise in arithmetic or simple algebra. Merely knowing that Billy needs to obtain an additional $5 tells us nothing about how he can actually go about obtaining it. Are Billy and his family poor? Does all the money that he earns go toward helping his family eat? If so, then the problem is how to help a family that is struggling financially to keep itself afloat. Arithmetic is of little help in solving this problem. A more relevant approach might be financial and family counseling for the whole family.

This is not to say that learning how to solve exercises is totally unimportant. It is merely to say that however they are taught, simple exercises are not the same as problems.

By "preformulated," we mean not only that the exercise is "completely given" to the student, but that all of the information necessary to solve it is completely specified as well. This means that everything confusing and extraneous has been artificially removed. As a result, the student does not learn how to formulate and to solve problems in the midst of confusion and noise, that is, extraneous and contradictory information. Indeed, confusion and noise are always fundamental parts of the broader environment in which all problems reside.

Suppose that every time Billy counts his money, he comes up with a different result. What then should the student conclude? That Billy doesn't know how to count? That's one possibility. But it's only one. There are many others, such as one of his siblings is "borrowing" money from him with or without his knowledge. Or, for another, that he has a "leaky" piggy bank or pants pocket.

Suppose by some miracle that Billy is a statistician; should he then just take the average of his various counts and regard it as the "best estimate" of the actual money he has? And if he did so, how would he use the information? Would it indeed be "information"?

The trouble with most textbooks and with education in general is that they assume that by giving students a steady diet of preformulated exercises, we help them to formulate and solve real, complex problems. Often, it only makes them want more of the same, in other words, more "canned exercises."

Another mistaken, and largely implicit, assumption is that real, complex problems generally can be decomposed into a series of simple and independent exercises. Thus the solution to an original problem is the *sum* of the *solutions* to the *separate exercises*. But, as the quote from Ackoff argues, a "problem" is the *product* of the *interactions* among the "parts" that make up a mess. The "solution," if there is one, is highly interactive as well. The solution is a function of the mess as a whole, not of any one of its parts.

Second, the exercise about Billy has one and only one solution. In this case, it is $5. This is one of the things that makes it into an exercise. Exercises thus convey the false impression that all problems have a single formulation and, as a result, a single solution.

Third, once solved, exercises remain solved. They are solved for everyone everywhere who understands the rules of the game, in this case, elementary arithmetic or simple algebra. Furthermore, everyone who understands arithmetic and algebra should get the same answer, $5. (This helps to explain the basis for the false assertion that "math and science are the only 'truly universal languages.'" A more accurate assertion is that "exercises are universally confused with problems.")

Four, exercises are usually the province of a single discipline. Every discipline has its own preferred textbooks. Very rarely do textbooks from different disciplines share the same problems. To solve shared problems, the student would have to apply and to integrate knowledge from two separate disciplines or fields of knowledge simultaneously. That is, the primary burden of integration is placed on the student and not on the instructors, who should have integrated their materials in the first place.

Finally, five, exercises instill another false lesson. An exercise can be defined clearly, precisely, and unambiguously, and *prior* to one's working on it. In addition, the definition is not supposed to vary as one works on the problem. The definition is not only supposed to be constant, but prior to the solution.

The end result is that students are turned into "certainty junkies." Anyone with teaching experience knows that they rebel like mad if they are given problems when they have been conditioned to expect exercises.

Problems have none of these characteristics.

For example, questions such as "Should the United States initially have invaded Iraq?" and "How should the United States extricate itself from Afghanistan?" are, to put it mildly, tortuous problems, and very different from simple-minded exercises.

First of all, problems are not preformulated. One of the biggest difficulties with problems is determining "exactly" what the problem is. Problem *formulation* is one of the key and most crucial aspects of problem *solving*. As an old saying puts it, "a problem well put is half solved." And, "he or she who controls the problem-setting agenda of a nation controls its destiny."

Two, problems have more than one solution precisely because they have more than one formulation. As Iraq and Afghanistan (not to mention health care) illustrate only too painfully, those with opposing political perspectives and ideologies don't see the issues the same way. Indeed, why should we expect them to?

Three, unlike exercises, problems are dynamic. They not only change as the circumstances change, they change in response to our so-called "solutions," that is, as a result of our working on them. More often than not, the solutions not only contribute to the problems, they actually make them worse. For instance, the war in Iraq has made the Middle East less, not more, stable.

Four, problems are not the exclusive province of any single discipline or profession. Although most people refer to it as such, the current financial crisis is not the sole or exclusive province of finance and economics.

Five, problems are inherently "messy." Take away the messiness and you take away what makes them problems. In fact, more often than not, taking away messiness not only makes problems worse, it makes their solutions more difficult, if not impossible, to obtain and to implement. Again, problems do not exist independently of the mess in which they are embedded. As a result, no problem can be solved independently of all the other problems to which it is connected.

Embedded in the fifth characteristic is another important difference between exercises and problems. In dealing with complex problems, typically, the definition(s) of the problems emerge only at the end of an inquiry, not at the beginning. If one really knows the definition of a problem prior to working on it, then it's not a true problem. As a result, the common admonitions to define the problem precisely and not to vary the definition of the problem are, strictly speaking, nonsense.

THE MOST GENERAL DEFINITION OF A PROBLEM

A problem exists when it is not clear that a set of presumably ethical means (for example, private health insurance versus government public health options) will achieve a desired set of presumably ethical ends (such as the general health and well-being of the entire U.S. population). A problem also exists when stakeholders disagree strongly on a set of ethical means to achieve a desired set of ethical ends. Figure 2.1 presents a typology of problems in terms of whether stakeholders agree or disagree over the means, the ends, or both.

A well-structured problem is a problem for which the means and the ends are both well known. Moreover, various stakeholders agree on the definition of the problem and that the means will achieve the ends. In addition, one's ethical stance and values are also well known and accepted by a "significant body" of stakeholders. In this case, the problem is to determine which of the means are the most efficient, are least costly, and involve the least time and effort in attaining the desired ends.

In contrast, an ill-structured problem is a problem for which either the means or the ends are unknown (and their effectiveness is in doubt) or for which there exists sharp and significant disagreement over what means should be employed to achieve what ends. In addition, one's ethical stance and values are in doubt or not well accepted by a "significant body" of stakeholders. In this case, the problem is to determine the nature of the problem, in other words, how to formulate it.

In a fundamental sense, all real problems worthy of the name have significant aspects that are ill structured.

Notice that there is a big difference between "means problems" and "ends problems." In the former case, presumably the ends are well known and accepted. The problem is then to discover or cre-

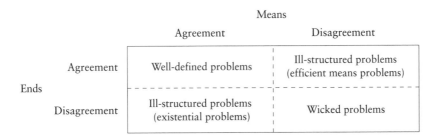

FIGURE 2.1. A typology of problems

Analytical or Technical

Well-defined, specific, independent causes and effects, clear definitions and boundaries, usually quantifiable and small aspects of "efficient *means* problems"	A system of ill-defined, fuzzy, messy, dynamically changing, and interdependent "ethical *means and ends* problems"
Well-defined, specific "existential problems" and "efficient *means* problems" of an individual or a small group of people Moral outrage, the feeling that there is something wrong with me, my family, and my immediate work group (or them)	A system of wicked, fuzzy, messy, dynamically changing, and interdependent "existential" and "ethical *means and ends* problems" of society or a large group Moral outrage, the feeling that there is something wrong with us or them or all of us, and with our ideals and the technologies and the organizations we created to achieve those ideals

Details   Whole

Personal or People

FIGURE 2.2. Problem types and psychological dispositions

ate the most efficient means for obtaining the ends. Such problems are termed "efficient means problems." For example, stakeholders may agree that financial crises must be prevented, but may disagree strongly over the means to achieve this: for example, what kind of regulations are appropriate, what is the role of free markets, when is direct government intervention warranted, and so on.

In the case of ends problems, one is charged with discovering or creating a set of ends around which people can coalesce. Such problems are best termed "existential problems." For example, various stakeholders may agree that investment banking is an indispensable part of the economy but they may disagree strongly over the core mission and purpose of investment banking. These problems are "existential" because the ends give meaning and purpose to those that are pursuing them. This is true even if the ends can never be fully attained. For instance, while we cannot eliminate wars at the present time, and perhaps never will, we still subscribe to the "ideal of finally eliminating all wars from the human condition." (An "ideal" is an end that we can never fully attain, but one that it is hoped we can "approach indefinitely." Ideals exist to give us meaning, purpose, and hope.)

The most extreme example of an ill-structured problem is a "wicked problem."[4] A wicked problem is a problem for which there appears to be no satisfactory way of determining an appropriate set of means or ends that would obtain sufficient agreement among a diverse set of stakeholders. No currently known discipline, profession, or body of knowledge is sufficient to define the "wickedly complex" nature of the problem. Iraq and Afghanistan more than fit the bill, and the health care crisis is very close, if not in the exact same ballpark.

Finally, take a look at Figure 2.2. In terms of the framework we introduced in Chapter 1, Figure 2.2 shows how the meaning of a problem varies in terms of one's underlying psychological disposition. For instance, those who prefer to take a complex whole and analyze its parts separately, and decide in an analytical and impersonal way, are attracted to well-defined problems. They tend not to question the ends and the means of a given problem. Rather they take them as exogenous constraints that must be satisfied to solve the problem (see the upper left quadrant in Figure 2.2). In contrast, those who prefer to look at large wholes and interconnections between parts, and decide in a values-based and more personal way, are attracted to wicked problems. They disagree with both the means and the ends imposed by the situation (see the lower right quadrant in Figure 2.2).

THE MEANINGS OF THE VERB "TO SOLVE"

Because most of us have been "trained," not "educated," on exercises, we also think that we know what it means to "solve" a problem. But problems do not have the same kinds of solutions that exercises do. To see this, let's take a look at the different meanings of the verb "to solve."

Suppose that a problem, P, exists whenever there is a significant gap between I, what we ideally would like to accomplish, and A, what we can currently accomplish. Thus, a problem $P = I - A > 0$. That is, a problem exists whenever P—the difference between our ideals, I, and our current abilities, A—is greater than zero.

Refer back to the simple example of Billy, who has $6 but needs $5 more in order to buy a game costing $11. In this case, $I = \$11$ and $A = \$6$. Thus, P equals $5. However, in terms of our earlier discussion, notice that by itself $P = \$5$ is not the problem. How to raise $5 is the problem, not the number itself.

To "solve" a problem P means to make $P = 0$, that is, $I = A$. We can do this in two different ways: one, by raising A up to I, and two, by lowering I to A. In the first case, we *raise* our actual abilities (means) up to our ideals (ends). In the second case, we *lower* our ideals (aspirations or ends) down to our abilities (means). If all stakeholders agree that the first or the second way is acceptable, then the problem is solved.

Notice that strictly speaking only exercises and well-structured problems have solutions such that $P = 0$. Ill-structured and wicked problems do not have solutions in this sense of the term. They are "coped with" and "managed," but never fully solved.

To "resolve" a problem means to contain it within acceptable limits. We no longer insist that $P = 0$, but instead that P be bounded within acceptable limits. For example, consider the rate of unemployment. According to economists, to attempt to make P = 0 by "solving" the problem of unemployment would be to create even worse economic and social problems, including a greater rate of future unemployment. So P = 0, or zero unemployment rate, is not a desired level. But an acceptable rate of unemployment for one stakeholder may not be acceptable to another. According to the Bureau of Labor Statistics, since the 1990s and until 2008, the unemployment rate in the United States was bounded within the range of 3.9 percent to 7.8 percent.[5]

To "dissolve" a problem means to lower or redefine its importance. When we dissolve a problem, we say that other problems within the system (the mess) in which the problem exists deserve our attention more. The problem P still exists within acceptable limits, but we shift our attention to other problems. The problem can be "managed properly" only by managing other problems within the mess. To "dissolve" a problem also means to redesign the system within which the problem is located. When the system is redesigned, it is hoped that the original problem no longer exists. Of course, a complete redesign of the system may create other kinds of messes.

To "absolve" a problem means to accept the fact that the problem P may never fully vanish. It may even grow worse over time. At best, it waxes and wanes. For example, it means accepting that problems such as terrorism are not "*wars that can be won*" but "*social diseases or pathologies* that can only be managed as best we can over time." This is a functional form of absolving because it leaves room for future resolutions or dissolutions.

However, the real essence of absolving is as follows: more often than not, we are committed to a pet solution or a series of pet solutions. In absolving, we work backward from our pet solution(s) to the definition(s) of a problem compatible with our preferred solution. But we do it in such a way that we make it appear that the definition of the problem came first. In other words, not only do we deny the existence or the messiness of our current problems, we take refuge in our need for solutions for well-defined problems. This form of absolving is dysfunctional because it is a form of "denial" (see Chapter 6), and it sends us down the path of solving the wrong problem precisely, which makes the current problems only worse. The overuse, underuse, or simply misuse of antibiotics is just one example. Another is encouraging U.S. consumers to borrow and to spend more and more, when in fact overspending and too much debt, which are clearly unsustainable in the long term, have been some of the main contributors to the current financial crisis. Overspending and too much debt are also manifestations of psychological defense mechanisms that save the day but prevent one from seeing the severity of the mess at hand.

Table 2.1 summarizes the argument so far.

TABLE 2.1. The differences between well-structured problems and ill-structured problems

Well-structured problems	Ill-structured problems
The problem is preformulated.	The problem is not preformulated.
Boundaries of problems are clear.	Boundaries of problems are fuzzy and part of the problem.
There is a single formulation and a single solution.	There are multiple formulations and multiple solutions, resolutions, dissolutions, and absolutions.
The definition of a problem does not vary as one works on the problem; the definition of a problem precedes its solution.	The definition(s) of the problem(s) change throughout the inquiry process.
The solution to a problem is the sum of the solutions to the separate parts.	The solution(s) to a problem is (are) a function of the mess as a whole, not any one of its parts.
The means and the ends are both well known.	The means and the ends are unknown.
Stakeholders agree on the definition of the problem and that the means will achieve the ends.	Stakeholders disagree on the definition of the problem and that the means will achieve the ends.
Once solved, problems remain solved.	Problems are dynamic; they change in response to our working on them.
Problems are usually the province of a single discipline or profession.	Problems are not the exclusive province of any single discipline or profession.

THE DEFINITION OF A MESS

Given all of the preceding concepts and definitions, we are finally able to give an expanded definition of a mess. A mess is the following:

1. A system of ill-defined or wicked problems interacting dynamically such that no problem can be abstracted from and analyzed independently of all the other problems that constitute the mess; in other words, none of the so-called "independent problems" or "parts" even exists independent of all the other problems or parts that constitute the mess and thus can't be analyzed; in somewhat different words, a mess is the product, not the sum, of the interactions between its parts (this part of the definition is from Ackoff)

2. The interactions between

   a. A complex and entangled web of stated and unstated, conscious and unconscious assumptions, beliefs, and values that underlie and enter into the problems that constitute a mess in Ackoff's terms

   b. A complex and entangled web of conscious and unconscious emotions that are part of and inevitably accompany any set of complex, messy, and important problems

   c. A complex and entangled web of "solutions" (resolutions, dissolutions, absolutions) that not only contribute to the mess but also are part of the mess

   d. A complex and entangled web of intended and unintended effects (consequences) that are the result of the problems and the entire mess itself; in this sense, the problems and the entire mess may be regarded as the "causes" of the "so-called effects"; the point is that what are regarded as "causes," "effects," "consequences," "problems," and "solutions" are all not only "conceptual abstractions" from the mess, but are part of the mess itself

e. A complex and entangled web of conundrums, counterintuitive ideas, paradoxes, puzzles, and surprises

f. A complex and entangled web of crises, about which we say much more in the succeeding chapters

All of the above and more constitute a mess.

THE FINANCIAL CRISIS

One of the most powerful and important examples of a mess is the current financial crisis. In most people's minds, the financial crisis encompasses the sequence of events that were triggered by the downturn in home prices. It is generally accepted that the crisis was felt first in the subprime mortgage market in 2007, and led to the bankruptcies of New Century Financial Corporation and American Home Mortgage Investment Corporation, J.P. Morgan's acquisition of Bear Stearns, significant and volatile drops in global asset markets, the bankruptcies of Lehman Brothers and Washington Mutual (among many others), the bailout of AIG, and several interventions of the Federal Reserve (hereafter, the Fed) and the Department of Treasury into the U.S. markets.

In the simplest possible terms, without explaining in detail the broader political, psychological, sociological, and historical contexts within which it is situated,[6] the financial crisis was due to the loosening of credit by the Fed, which was heavily lobbied by the banking industry to relax credit and banking restrictions so that the industry could make more money. In other words, the banking industry that is overseen by the Fed exerted strong pressure on the Fed to do its bidding.

The loosening of credit, which is one of the tools the Fed used (misused and abused, according to some) to soften contractions in the economy, in turn contributed strongly to the inflating of a housing bubble. This meant that too many people were given loans and mortgages that they could not afford. In far too many cases, unscrupulous loan officers were pressured by the unscrupulous lending institutions for which they worked to make as many loans as possible.

The banks and Wall Street not only made money on the initial loan transactions, they then made money repeatedly when the mortgages were bundled together and rebundled and sold over and over again to retirement funds and even to the same Wall Street firms that originated them. In effect, the institutions that originated highly risky products bought their own toxic products. In addition, insurance policies were developed on the risky bundles (toxic products) such that if anywhere along the chain one person or institution defaulted on repayment of the loans, the person or institution holding the policies would receive the monies for which the policies were written. Of course, these financial products were not regulated or monitored properly, and hence became additional toxic products in their own right.

The trouble began when home prices started to go down and the initial "low teaser rates" on mortgages were reset to higher rates and monthly loan payments shot up. As a result, people who should not have received loans and mortgages in the first place were neither able to repay the loans nor able to refinance them. And because of the drop in home prices, they weren't able to sell their homes and cash out, either, as they used to do in the past. This started a chain reaction of defaults because the banks and other lending institutions had not set aside enough capital to cover the payments of the insurance policies in case there were mass defaults. In short, there was not enough liquid capital to keep the system going. Ironically, too much of it, in the form of credit, was a main cause of this crisis in the first place. Even more ironically, even more of it, in the form of bailouts, lower Fed funds rates, and other unconventional tools such as TARP, has been the Fed's solution to it.

Although we refer to the mess as "the financial crisis," we do not want to focus our attention only on the financial aspects of the crisis. The attempt to understand the mess solely through a financial or an economic lens is doomed to fail. In fact, doing so only contributes more to the failure to find solutions, assuming of course that there are "true solutions."

Figure 2.3 is a "partial" illustration of the many aspects or components of the financial crisis as a mega-mess. But note that these components cannot be understood by using a finance or economics perspective only.

FIGURE 2.3. A "partial" illustration of the financial crisis as a mega-mess

A few features deserve special mention, for they bring out additional aspects that are found in virtually all messes. One, the figure is far from complete. Many more boxes could be added to it, ad infinitum. Indeed, by definition, how could it ever be complete? Thus a prime component in dealing with messes is the psychological necessity of a high tolerance for ambiguity, or as we would put it, a high tolerance for messiness. If this tolerance is lacking, then one will invariably seek to reduce the messiness and as a result make the mess worse.

Two, each of the "separate boxes or factors" can be expanded and analyzed indefinitely. There are boxes, factors, and variables within boxes, factors, and variables. In this sense, there are no "natural ending points" in analyzing messes.

Three, one can start (enter) and end (exit) the mess at any point. There is no preferred starting or stopping point. In other words, there is no final direction of causality. An arrow can be drawn in either direction between any two or more boxes, factors, or variables. Furthermore, the "arrows" represent the interactions between each of the "components" of the mess, whether they be problems, assumptions, consequences, or so on.

Although there obviously are prior historical factors and forces that operate, one can also run the picture backward to see how today's factors and forces lead one to understand better the past and the "causes" of future crises. Another way to put it is to say that every mess loops back within itself. In this sense, every mess can be run forward and backward. There is no preferred direction, as it were.

Four, intense emotions are always present throughout even if they are not always shown explicitly in one of the boxes. To be sure, they undergird the entire diagram. Consider:

A national survey of jobless workers . . . shows just how traumatized the work force has become. . . . Two-thirds of respondents said that they had become depressed. More than half said it was the first time they had ever lost a job, and 89 percent said there was little or no chance that they would be able to get their jobs back when the economy improves.[7]

ASSUMPTIONS

Let us summarize how Figures 2.2 and 2.3 and Table 2.1 fit together. Consider the following two questions:

1. Should the components of Figure 2.3 be tackled one by one or simultaneously?

2. Should President Obama have decided to tackle one and only one major problem at a time, for instance, the financial crisis? Or was he fundamentally correct in tackling a whole host of problems (or "the mess") simultaneously: health care, the Afghan War, and so on?

If one's psychological disposition fits the profile shown in the upper left quadrant of Figure 2.2 (detail/technical/analytical), then one tends to believe that the financial crisis is only a "financial" crisis; its handling is best left to experts (with experience or PhDs in economics or finance); it is a relatively well-structured problem (see Table 2.1); and some of the components in Figure 2.3 are irrelevant and the relevant ones should be tackled one by one.

If one's psychological disposition fits the profile shown in the lower right quadrant of Figure 2.2 (whole/personal /people), then one tends to believe that the crisis is a system of crises, including a financial crisis; that its handling is better not left to experts but to a diverse group of representatives from as many disciplines and professions as possible; that it is an ill-structured, wicked problem (see Table 2.1); and that all of the components in Figure 2.3 and more are relevant and they should be tackled simultaneously.

However one answers, there obviously are grave implications. But precisely because the answers are so grave, they reveal underlying assumptions about what one thinks the world basically is and should be like.

If you answered that President Obama should have tackled only one major problem at a time, then in effect you assumed something like the following:

1. The vast majority of people have a very limited attention span; as a consequence, they can only focus on a limited

number of problems at any point in time; focusing on more than one problem will only confuse and even anger them, as we have seen in the recent Town Hall meetings and demonstrations against government-run health care.

2. Focusing on more than one problem only dilutes our already limited resources and energy as a nation.

3. While many, if not most, problems obviously affect one another, we can still treat them as though they are essentially independent; therefore, the overall solution to all of our problems is the sum of the solutions to the separate problems taken one at a time; in other words, problems can be decoupled and treated separately.

If, however, you answered that President Obama was fundamentally correct in tackling more than one problem at a time, then in effect you assumed something like the following:

1. None of our "major problems" are independent of one another anymore; in fact, they haven't been independent for a long time.

2. None of our major problems can be "defined," let alone "solved," independent of one another because they don't exist independently.

3. The problems we face are parts of larger messes.

4. The sooner we teach people how to tolerate and to appreciate messes, the better off all of us will be. How to change the system of education to accomplish this is another mess!

5. The solution to a mess is a function of the product of the interactions among all of its parts.

6. You don't "solve" messes; you confront and cope with them as best you can.

CONCLUDING REMARKS

At this point, readers may wonder, rightfully so, whether it is possible to study and understand "messes" or complex systems of problems. In Part II and Part III, we will outline the proper philosophical base and methodology for studying messes. For now it is sufficient to say that no preference is to be given to any academic discipline or profession in explaining or understanding any mess. Indeed, the failures of the economics and finance disciplines and professions to predict the financial mess, and to accept that many of the theories of economics and finance were directly responsible for the crisis, are themselves parts of the mess. Given the violence that was done to those on Wall Street who lost their jobs and to those on Main Street who lost their retirement accounts, plus the child and spousal abuse that occurred as the result of those who lost their jobs in the general economy, the financial crisis must be understood both as an economic and financial crisis *and* as a public health crisis, that is, a crisis of violence. In this way the financial system is not only a "financial spreading" system, it is also a "violence spreading" system. If there are any doubts about the connection between finance and violence, then the following should dispel them:

Associated Press Writer Juliet Williams, September 8, 2009.
SACRAMENTO, Calif.—Six domestic violence shelters in California have been forced to close while dozens more are scaling back services after Gov. Arnold Schwarzenegger eliminated all state funding for the program that supports them.

Because it helps to understand messes better, let us examine the link between the financial crisis and violence. Once again, we know that whenever there are severe financial downturns, spousal and child abuse go up dramatically. In a word, people take out their frustrations on the most vulnerable "elements" of their immediate world. Thus financial crises and child abuse are linked directly. Not only are the interactions between them strong, the greater the severity of a downturn, the greater the increase in spousal and child abuse. But are they also linked in other ways? Does the arrow of causality run in the opposite direction as well? Does greater abuse somehow lead to greater financial crises?

The answers to all are "Yes!"

In an extremely important book, *Liquidated*,[8] anthropologist Karen Ho shows how the violence (abuse) that is perpetuated on those who work on Wall Street is a significant factor in the creation of major financial crises. That is, the systematic abuse of those who work on Wall Street leads to financial crises. Here's how it operates.

For the most part, new hires are recruited mainly from four elite universities: Harvard, Princeton, Yale, and The Wharton School of the University of Pennsylvania. The graduates of these prestigious schools make up the bulk of those who work on Wall Street, and especially those who make it to "the top." In short, the "best and the brightest" only hire those in their own image.

But then the cycle of violence begins.

New hires are worked like indentured slaves between 100 and 140 hours a week. But since you are only as good as your last big deal, and deals don't always work out, the chances of failure are extremely high. The chances of being fired are extremely high as well. The result? The vast majority of people on "The Street" are "liquidated" frequently.[9]

The constant pressure to perform means that one continually has to sell deals to corporate America that result in big profits. During the 1990s, this led to huge waves of large mergers and acquisitions, or M and A's. The M and A's brought huge profits to Wall Street brokers who sold the deals. But when companies merged, corporate America laid off large numbers of people that they didn't need anymore. The fact that those selling the deals were themselves liquidated constantly led them to feel little if any compunction about their own actions that led to the "liquidation" of others.

In this way, the circle is complete: Do Unto Others What Has Been Done to Us! In short, violence begets violence.

Consider the "religious" and, particularly, the "fundamentalist" aspects.[10] In the *New York Times*, Barbara Ehrenreich and Dedrick Muhammad wrote,

Elizabeth Jacobson, a former loan officer at [Wells Fargo], recently revealed—in an affidavit in a lawsuit by the city of Baltimore—that salesmen were encouraged to try to persuade black preachers to hold "wealth-building seminars" in their churches. For every loan that resulted from these seminars, whether to buy a new home or to refinance them, Wells Fargo promised to donate $350 to the customer's favorite charity, usually the church. . . . Another former loan officer, Tony Paschal, reported that cynicism was rampant within Wells Fargo, with some employees referring to subprimes as "ghetto loans" and to minority customers as "mud people."

If any cultural factor predisposed blacks to fall for risky loans, it was one widely shared with whites—a penchant for "positive thinking" and unwarranted optimism, which takes the theological form of the "prosperity gospel." Since "God wants to prosper you," all you have to do to get something is "name it and claim it." A 2000 DVD from the black evangelist Creflo Dollar featured African-American parishioners shouting, "I want my stuff right now!"[11]

The point is that if you truly want to understand something as big and as complicated as the financial system, then you can't just look in all the obvious places. You have to understand and to manage it as a mess.

The moral is that if you really want to prevent future financial crises, then you have to change (or "dissolve") the entire system by which people are hired, the day-to-day conditions under which they work, and how they are rewarded. Anything less just perpetuates and reinforces the current system.

If we focus on just one or two of the obvious parts of a mess, and if we attempt to isolate them from the other parts, then we inevitably end up solving the wrong problems precisely. Nothing perpetuates a mess like solving the wrong problems precisely.

Seeing something as complex as the financial crisis as a mess helps to see other things that would escape our attention if we saw it only as a financial or an economic crisis.

With these concepts and ideas in mind, we are ready to turn to mega-crises as mega-messes.

3 ALL CRISES ARE MESSES

The truth is that [large-scale organizational] change is inherently messy. It is always complicated. It invariably involves a massive array of sharply conflicting demands. Despite the best-laid plans, things never happen in exactly the right order—and in fact, few things rarely turn out exactly right the first time around. Most important, the reality of change in the organizational trenches defies rigid academic models as well as superficial management fads.

— DAVID NADLER, *Champions of Change*

ALL CRISES ARE MESSES because of three highly related factors. First, stakeholders who are affected not only define crises differently, they have intense disagreements over what is happening and why, what is known versus unknown, who is responsible, whom to trust, what needs to be done, and so on. In fact, the variations in the various stakeholders' definitions, assumptions, and perspectives provide strong clues about the messiness of the crisis.

Second, all crises are messes because they contain a wide variety of issues, problems, and assumptions that cannot be dealt with separately. All of the issues, problems, and assumptions that constitute a mess must be dealt with simultaneously.

Third, crises also are messy because they are not single isolated events. An initial crisis always and quickly, if not simultaneously, triggers a chain reaction of other crises. In fact, one might argue that if a crisis did not trigger other crises, then it was not a crisis to begin with.

This chapter also demonstrates that while not all messes are necessarily crises, because of their complex and dynamic nature, and the potential to mismanage them, all messes have the possibility of turning into crises.

In sum, all crises are complex systems of multiple, interacting, and interdependent crises, all of which can and will be viewed differently by different stakeholders. If crises are not treated and managed systemically, then the messiness of the initial crisis will grow exponentially.

THE MEGA-MESS THAT IS U.S. HEALTH CARE

In this chapter, we want to use the health care crisis to demonstrate that all crises are messes. Unfortunately, it is also one of the best examples one could use to illustrate that all messes have the potential to turn into multiple crises, that is, mega-crises.

The Myers-Briggs framework we introduced in Chapter 1 is especially helpful for it reveals four general stakeholder perspectives on the health care crisis. As shown in Figures 3.1 and 3.2, each perspective (or quadrant) shows not only different but conflicting aspects of the crisis. First, consider Figure 3.1.

The upper left and upper right quadrants both deal with costs, but in very different ways. The upper left quadrant assumes not only that the health care system can be broken down into separate parts and that the costs associated with each part (different treatments, individual specialists, and so on) can be determined independently of the other parts and the whole system, but that it *must* be broken down if one is to be able to analyze health care properly. In slightly different words, the upper left quadrant assumes that if the problems associated with health care are not broken down into separate parts, then the overall problems cannot be properly addressed.

Fear of Spiraling
Costs/Loss of Control

Fear of Systems Collapse

Analytical or Technical

Cost containment	*Innovation*
The system can be broken down and analyzed as separate parts.	The whole is different from the sum of its parts.
How will we contain the cost of health care?	How can we redesign the total system?
$1 trillion	$35 trillion
Personal concerns	*Societal values*
The health care system must solve the unique problems of particular individuals.	Health care is not a business or a consumer product. It is a fundamental human right.
Am I getting the best treatment for my condition? Can I afford it? Can my family afford it?	We ought to ensure health for all.

Parts

Whole

Personal Fears

Personal or People

Fear of Societal Collapse

FIGURE 3.1.   Four general perspectives on health care

In the upper left quadrant, the fear of changing the health care system as a whole and all at once is grounded in the basic assumption that big changes are obtained only through small, concrete, incremental, and deliberate changes in each of the individual parts. These changes come about as the result of local experiments, small process enhancements, efforts to eliminate ambiguities and contradictions in the protocols for delivering care, and so on.[1] In other words, big changes are warranted only if they are grounded in small, deliberate, and careful changes to each of the individual parts that are backed up and confirmed by "hard data." Indeed, unless one has hard data to back up one's ideas and proposals, then changes are not warranted at all.

In contrast, the upper right quadrant assumes that one must have a sense of the overall system *as a system* before any action is warranted. What is a "legitimate" part can only be decided in terms of the context of the whole system. For example, the true costs of health care must be computed across the entire spectrum of care. Thus the costs associated with the treatment of, say, a bacterial infection must be computed across all the aspects of dealing with it, from the first time that patients see a physician until the time the infection is completely treated. The costs associated with this treatment include visits to subsequent specialists and all of the follow-up procedures, as well as the costs of creating new drugs to treat bacteria that become resistant to current antibiotic drugs. In other words, the true costs of health care are systemic. As a result, they cannot be addressed fully by local and isolated efforts alone. Instead, they need to be addressed by a variety of systemic innovations such as universal coverage, market-based pricing, and single payer or consumer-driven systems.[2]

Notice that whereas the upper left quadrant focuses on the parts of the current system and what we can do right now to fix them, the upper right quadrant focuses on designing future systems. In the upper right quadrant, the fear of failing to use systemic innovations to change the health care system is grounded in the assumption that the whole is either greater or smaller than the sum of its parts, and that by only addressing the parts, one will invariably make the problem(s) worse. (The whole is greater if the interactions among the parts are positively correlated; it is smaller if the interactions are negatively correlated.)

To take another example, the upper left quadrant worries about the projected cost to U.S. taxpayers of $900 billion to $1 trillion if we move to government-sponsored health care, and what it will add to the already huge deficits. In contrast, the upper right quadrant worries about the huge increases in individual health premiums that are estimated at some $35 trillion over the next decade if we don't have a systemic redesign such as government-aided health care.

The lower left and lower right quadrants have completely different but equally legitimate takes on the crisis.

The lower left quadrant focuses solely on individuals because everyone is unique and therefore experiences health care differently. The primary concern is, "What will the current and any future system do to me, my immediate family, and close friends?" The lower left quadrant assumes that a proper response to the health care mess cannot be made without an understanding of the unique circumstances (preexisting conditions, lifetime caps, rescissions, early retirement, and so on) of particular individuals and how they will end up making choices about their health care needs.

In contrast, the lower right quadrant focuses on the larger social, political, and moral questions surrounding health care. What does the current state of the health care system reveal about our society as a whole? Isn't health care a "fundamental human right," not a "business"? And, if it is a "right," who should pay for it and how? Does society have a moral responsibility to provide health care for everyone no matter what the cost? Or do individuals have a moral responsibility to take good care of themselves? Where do the responsibilities of society end and the responsibilities of individuals begin? (Is this even the right question to ask?) What is the proper role of government? To be sure, progressives and conservatives answer these questions in diametrically opposed ways. For example, whereas progressives identify government as a part of the solution to the health care crisis, conservatives tend to identify it as a part of the problem. In sum, the lower right quadrant assumes that we cannot make a proper response to the health care mess without acknowledging and confronting fundamental social, moral, and political decisions that influence it and, even more to the point, in which it is embedded.

In short, the left quadrants believe that health care can be addressed by breaking the mess apart into its separate components, whether the "components" are individual problems in the case of the upper left or problems of unique individuals in the case of the lower left. The overall solution to health care is thus the sum of the solutions to the separate problems.

In sharp contrast, the right quadrants believe that health care is a mess and must be addressed as such, that is, as a complex, messy system that cannot, and therefore, must not be "broken apart." Messes cannot be fully addressed by solving individual problems or the problems of individuals separately. Thus we need to abandon altogether the notion that individual problems can be even formulated, let alone solved, independent of one another. In other words, messes need to be managed systemically. The solutions, if there are any, are a function—property—of the entire mess as a whole.

Proper management of the health care mess needs to address all four perspectives simultaneously and equitably. The contributions and cooperation of many stakeholders are required not only during the formulation of the mess but also during the implementation of agreed-upon courses of action. This is not an easy task. As Figure 3.2 shows, each quadrant has a very different definition of health care and therefore a very different approach to it. For example, stakeholders that favor the upper left quadrant are concerned more with the treatment or prevention of a disease at the level of individual components, patients, hospitals, cities, and so on, whereas those that favor the upper right quadrant are concerned more with the treatment or prevention of a disease at the level of the entire health care system.

In the upper quadrants, health is defined as the "absence of illness," both at the individual and population level. Most people

Analytical or Technical

Health as "absence of illness" at the patient level Affordable health care	Health as "absence of illness" at the population level Sustainable health care system
Health as "presence of wellness" at the personal level High-quality health care	Health as "presence of wellness" at the community level Health care system accessible to all

Parts (left)   Whole (right)

Personal or People

FIGURE 3.2.   Four general definitions and goals of health care

would very likely agree with this. But what counts as illness? There are various markers or indicators associated with various types of illnesses. As a result, medical tests may or may not reveal that individuals or entire populations don't have such illnesses. But is this sufficient evidence to argue that they are healthy? Not necessarily.

The lower quadrants have a different but complementary definition. Health is the "presence of wellness." Thus the lower left focuses on the well-being of individuals, whereas the lower right is concerned with the wellness of entire communities. The lower quadrants also recognize that at least part of what we call "healthy" is socially constructed and depends on the values of the society. For instance, take obesity. While what is considered a healthy body weight has been decreasing in some societies, obesity is seen as a sign of health in others. Thus absence of disease and presence of wellness do not always mean the same thing.

Notice also that the quadrants contain multiple and often conflicting but equally valid goals such as affordability, high quality, long-term sustainability, and accessibility. Once again, not only do the quadrants have different goals, the definitions of key terms are different depending upon the particular quadrant. For instance, "high quality" is not the same in each quadrant.

In brief, our overview and analysis of the health care crisis, as well as Figures 3.3 and 3.4, show that different, conflicting aspects of the crisis and general perspectives with respect to health care are located in different quadrants. Of course, there is more to the story than is included in our discussion. But the point is this: none of the quadrants by itself is sufficient to deal with the crisis. If particular stakeholders have a natural tendency to see, and therefore to analyze, the crisis from one and only one perspective, they will invariably miss other important perspectives, thereby potentially making the crisis messier and its overall treatment worse. Figures 3.1 and 3.2 thus illustrate the multidimensional, systemic, and messy nature of the health care crisis, and by extension, all crises.

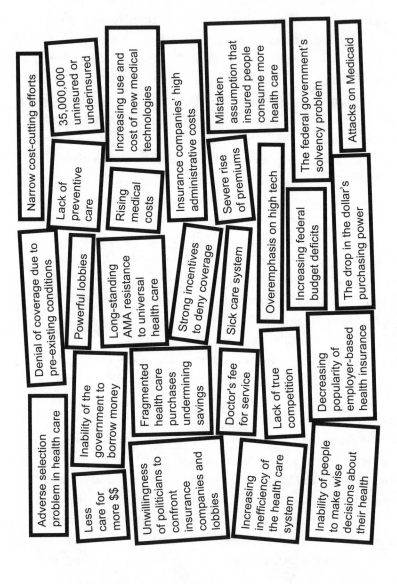

FIGURE 3.3. The long-standing health care mess

SOME OF THE MESSY ISSUES OF
THE HEALTH CARE CRISIS

The previous section has provided a framework and several examples to illustrate four general and fundamentally different perspectives on the health care crisis. This section demonstrates that health care consists of a multitude of issues and problems that are so interrelated they cannot be addressed without considering all of them.

Figure 3.3 shows some of the traditional or long-standing issues and problems involved in health care. As such, Figure 3.3 represents the "traditional mess" that has been and is U.S. health care. One can use arrows to draw lines from each box in Figure 3.3 to all of the others. This demonstrates how all of them are interrelated. But the real purpose is to be able to construct plausible stories or scenarios about the possible relationships between them. For example, it is not hard to imagine scenarios that connect "powerful lobbies," "severe rise of premiums," and "lack of true competition."

Figure 3.4 is a simplified diagram that shows how the longer-standing health care debate, or the "traditional mess," in Figure 3.3 has been embedded, at least at the time of the writing of this book, in a relatively new mess. The newer mess in Figure 3.4 is in part a result of the often noisy and highly disruptive demonstrations against the increased role of government in health care. These demonstrations erupted at public forums around the United States, especially those that were convened by senators and congresspeople home on August recess in 2009.

Figure 3.4 reveals a much more dangerous and ominous side to the issue. This is not to deny that Figure 3.3 contains a number of highly disturbing and ominous features as well. For one, it is estimated by the Employee Benefit Research Institute that up to 45,000,000 Americans have no health care insurance.[3] For another, it is also estimated that as a result, 35,000 people die annually because they do not have adequate coverage. Three, and perhaps most troubling of all, these two numbers are not disturbing to many people. Nonetheless, Figure 3.4 shows a more overtly violent and ugly side to the mess. The eminent, Pulitzer Prize–winning historian Richard Hofstadter captured

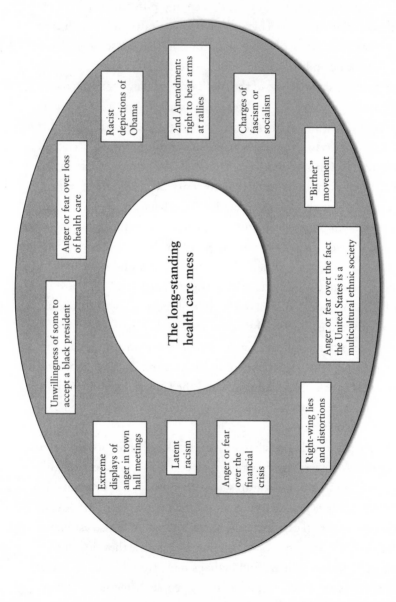

FIGURE 3.4. The recent health care mess

this side in his celebrated work on the "paranoid style of American politics."[4] Important issues in U.S. history have always brought to the surface a deeply disturbing and dark side of American politics.

The embeddedness of Figure 3.3 in Figure 3.4 is very important. Figure 3.3 represents a set of "cognitive" conflicts among the stakeholders of the health care system. Cognitive conflicts are functional disagreements over the ideas and issues at hand; they are not personal. For example, each of the four quadrants in Figures 3.1 and 3.2 presents a set of ideas and issues about which stakeholders may disagree. These types of conflicts, when analyzed and debated properly, tend to improve stakeholders' understanding of the issues, and the quality of the outcome or the final decision.[5]

Figure 3.4, however, represents a set of "affective" or emotional conflicts among stakeholders. Affective conflicts can be highly dysfunctional. They tend to focus on incompatibilities. They are perceived as personal criticisms. These types of conflicts, when not managed properly, tend to lower not only the quality of the outcome or the decision[6] but also the commitment to the decision as well as its implementation effectiveness.[7]

To appreciate the messiness of health care, one only needs to acknowledge that each of the separate issues and problems identified in Figures 3.3 and 3.4 can be analyzed further using the four Myers-Briggs perspectives, and that each of these separate issues and problems can potentially lead to cognitive and affective conflicts among stakeholders.

Because most people use one or two perspectives to focus only on a subset of these issues, it is a good mental and emotional exercise for readers to pick one issue from Figure 3.3 or 3.4, view it from all four Myers-Briggs perspectives, and think of all possible ways that the issue is connected to some of the others.

THE U.S. HEALTH CARE MEGA-CRISIS

We want to turn now to an analysis of U.S. health care as a mega-crisis: a complex system of multiple, interacting, and interdependent crises. To see this, consider Table 3.1.

TABLE 3.1. Major crisis types

Breaks	Outbreaks	Psychopathic or criminal	Economic	Human resources	Reputational	Informational	Natural hazards
Loss of key equipment, plants, or supplies	Epidemics	Product tampering	Labor strikes	Loss of key executives or personnel	Slander	Loss of proprietary and confidential information	Earthquakes
Breakdown of key equipment, or plants	Pandemics	Kidnapping	Labor unrest	Rise in absenteeism	Gossip	False information	Fires
Loss of key facilities		Hostage taking	Labor shortage	Rise in vandalism and accidents	Sick jokes	Tampering with computer records	Floods
Major plant disruption		Terrorism	Major decline in stock price and fluctuations	Workplace violence	Rumors	Loss of key stakeholder information	Typhoons
Explosions		Workplace violence	Market crash		Damage to corporate reputation		Hurricanes
			Decline in major earnings		Tampering with corporate logos		
			Recessions				
			Depressions				

Table 3.1 gives a brief typology of crises.[8] Previous research has shown that there are a relatively small number of different clusters, families, or types of crises such as "economic," "informational," or "psychopathic or criminal."[9] Table 3.1 also gives some brief examples of the different subtypes of crises in each of the various families.[10]

One of the most important results from previous research is that as far as we know, *no crisis* has been found to be a single, well-defined crisis that is contained solely within one and only one cluster or family. That is, *every* crisis is a *system* of multiple crises. *Every* crisis literally is in at least two or more families simultaneously. This happens because either the initial crisis consists of multiple crises in two or more families to begin with or the initial crisis sets off a chain reaction of other crises. Any particular type of crisis, or crises, is (are) capable of serving as the cause, the effect, or both of any other crisis or crises.

The economic aspects (subcrises) of health care are obvious and rampant throughout Figures 3.3 and 3.4. If one interprets, as progressive politicians do, the denial of coverage of those who have purchased health insurance and who have paid all of their premiums on time as a form of "psychopathic or criminal behavior on the part of the insurance companies," then from their perspective the crisis automatically belongs to more than one crisis family. That is, it is simultaneously an economic and a criminal crisis. (Indeed, some progressives argue that the insurance companies have practiced a form of "death squads" by denying treatment for those who have paid their premiums in full.) Thus, if only from this perspective, the mess that is health care both enhances and spreads paranoia. Certainly from the perspective of Richard Hofstadter,[11] the "psychopathic or criminal" subcrises of health care as shown in Figure 3.4 are immediately prominent. Whether one agrees with this interpretation or not, the health care industry has at a minimum a huge PR crisis on its hands. If only from this standpoint, the crisis is not a single crisis.

Consider other types of crises that the health care crisis can trigger. For example, one of the proposed solutions to the health care crisis is a "consumer-directed" option. The fear lurking behind this proposal is that if someone else picks up the bill, then people will consume more health care. Therefore, the "solution" to this potential crisis is that people should pay more for health insurance and pick up more of their expenses. First of all, the solution is not supported by the available research.[12] Second, forcing people to pay more for their medical expenses may help contain costs in the short run, but unless people are educated to make decisions intelligently and to learn how to manage health properly, in the long term, such solutions may actually be more costly, if not deadly, thereby turning the health care crisis into different forms of economic as well as legal and moral crises.

In short, the health care crisis is not only a mega-mess but also a mega-crisis, that is, a system of interacting crises. As explained in the following section, treating it as anything less is nothing but an invitation to get more of a mega-mess and mega-crisis.

A PARADOX

Our discussion of the health care mess suggests that if any mess is not managed properly, then not only can it become messier, it may eventually turn into a crisis.

Even though by definition a "mess" is a system of highly interactive, dynamically changing, ill-structured problems, assumptions, causes, effects, emotions, and so on, the time scale in which the elements of a mess change is significant.[13] A "stable mess" is one for which the interactions are relatively stable, whereas an "unstable mess" is one in which things are changing more rapidly than the mess can be studied. Messes also differ in terms of how intelligible or unintelligible they are. An "unintelligible mess" is one in which the gap between the skills and knowledge of those charged with studying and managing it widens over time. In contrast, an "intelligible mess" is one for which a set of stakeholders have the relevant interdisciplinary skills and knowledge to study and to manage the mess.

Messes that become unstable, unintelligible, or both are early warning signals of impending crises. Such early warning signals are more about us than they are about messes, for they get to the heart of how we deal with messes.

It is our contention that messes tend to have the following paradoxical property: Messes that are managed as if they are stable or intelligible have the tendency to become unstable or unintelligible over time, while messes that are managed as if they are unstable or unintelligible have the tendency to become more stable or intelligible over time.

To manage a mess as if it is stable or intelligible is to deal with a few aspects of it and to view it primarily from the perspective of only one quadrant of the Myers-Briggs framework. Consider health care again. Most people would agree that the health care mess has at least four broad problem themes: delivery or access, quality, financing, and sustainability. Focusing on only one of these themes (such as redesigning or modifying the financial aspects of health care) without considering its interactions with the other themes is to make fundamental assumptions about how the health care system as a whole works. More important, it makes assumptions about any number of stakeholders who were not included in the analysis. Not only is it a reductionist approach that decreases the stability or the intelligibility of the mess, it is also the exact opposite of what needs to be done: to bring to the surface and confront one's own assumptions about the mess.

To manage a mess as if it is unstable or unintelligible is to deal with as many aspects as possible by viewing it from the perspectives of all four quadrants of the Myers-Briggs framework. It is to bring to the surface and test taken-for-granted assumptions of as many stakeholders as possible. It is also the right way to manage a mess.

CONCLUDING REMARKS

If one uses both the traditional and the expanded definitions of a crisis that we presented in Chapter 1, then it can easily be seen that every crisis is indeed a multiple crisis. For instance, every crisis has the potential for adverse economic impacts. Every crisis has the potential for adverse media coverage and therefore adverse PR, and so on. While this does not of course prove that all crises are mega-crises, it strongly suggests that while all crises are messes, not all messes are necessarily crises. On the other hand, it also suggests that because of their sheer complexity and highly volatile nature, all messes have the potential to become crises and to produce multiple crises.

The preceding has strong implications for practice. It says that one *must never* prepare crisis plans and procedures or conduct training sessions in isolation. Instead, one needs to prepare for the simultaneous occurrence of multiple crises. This means that the crisis plans, procedures, and preparations for *any* single crisis must as much as possible be done in conjunction with *all other* crises. In other words, crisis plans must be prepared jointly, that is, interactively, and not independently. Indeed, one of the biggest assumptions, if not the biggest, that this chapter challenges is that crises are independent and therefore can be planned for and managed as such.

This chapter also forces us to bring to the surface, test, and challenge constantly as many assumptions about ourselves, our organizations and institutions, and our technologies as we can. For instance, one needs to consider how the latest technologies can actually make us more, not less, vulnerable. Having access to the most advanced medical technologies is not the same as being healthy or delivering the best health care.

One must also consider the faulty assumptions that can cause the crises in one type in Table 3.1 to contribute to the crises in all of the other types. To use a single example, one needs to consider how economic belt-tightening such as laying off employees in health care can set off incidents of workplace violence and tampering with confidential patient information. Thus, for every one of the crisis types in Table 3.1, one needs to consider the assumptions that one is making about why a particular crisis in one type will or will not set off a particular crisis or a set of crises in all of the other types.

We cannot emphasize too strongly that one of the primary purposes for looking at messes is not to analyze each of the component parts in detail but to gain a sense of the whole such that those interactions between the parts that are of special interest can be singled out. Above all, the purpose of this chapter has been to demonstrate how tools such as the Myers-Briggs framework can be used to expose those parts and interactions that ordinary analyses tend to overlook. This chapter also reminds us that providing a partial, incomplete solution to the whole is better than providing a complete solution to the parts.

Finally, this chapter warns us that improperly managed messes turn into crises. To manage a mess improperly is to assume that it is stable and intelligible and to pay attention to only a few aspects of it. To manage a mess properly is to assume that it is unstable and unintelligible and to pay attention to as many aspects of it as possible. The strongest conclusion is that if we treat today's messes and crises as if they are stable and intelligible, the messes of the future will be relatively more unstable and more unintelligible.

In the succeeding chapters, we will say a lot more about how the ideas of this chapter can be put to use in managing mega-messes and mega-crises.

4 WHEN GOOD ORGANIZATIONS DO UNWISE, IMMATURE, AND BAD THINGS

WASHINGTON (AP)—Bids topped $10,000 Thursday on an Internet auction site for what an animal rights group says are notes from football star Michael Vick's speech apologizing for a dogfighting scandal.

The Humane Society of the United States is selling on eBay the single-page, six-point outline of the speech Vick gave at an Aug. 27 [2007] news conference in Richmond after pleading guilty in his dogfighting case.

—SUZANNE GAMBOA, *Associated Press*, September 6, 2007

IN DEALING WITH MESSES AND CRISES, managers often make a serious mistake. They fail to bring to the surface and challenge the assumptions they hold about themselves and their stakeholders. The aim of this chapter is to understand why this occurs. In particular, why do managers at ostensibly good organizations make faulty assumptions and, as a result, get suckered into doing the wrong things, thereby causing a crisis for themselves and others?

We argue that this happens for at least two reasons: the inability to manage effectively the conflicts and tension between their emotions and moral values and the inability to take the perspectives of other stakeholders. These two factors are parts of what is commonly referred to as emotional intelligence.[1] We explore the role of these two factors in aiding and abetting crises and messes.

The chapter also illustrates some of the key ideas of the previous chapter in that it illuminates some of the most crucial assumptions that organizations all too often make about themselves and other stakeholders. Finally, it not only shows how every crisis is a multiple set of crises, but that every crisis is thereby a mess.

A CARDINAL RULE OF CRISIS MANAGEMENT

One of the cardinal rules of crisis management is, never, never, never underestimate the capacity of *all* organizations—but especially good ones—to do unwise, immature, and bad things!

A classic example is the following. In granting the wishes of terminally ill children, the Make-A-Wish Foundation is without a doubt one of the most commendable organizations ever founded. In fact, we would argue that granting the wishes of terminally ill children is one of the best examples of one's ability to empathize with or take the perspective of others.

In May 1996, the *Los Angeles Times* published an article in which it reported that the Foundation made the decision to grant the wish of a terminally ill child who was suffering from an inoperable brain tumor.[2] Fortunately, the child later survived.

The child wanted to fly to Alaska so that he could shoot a Kodiak bear. If that in itself wasn't shocking enough, and furthermore, that an upstanding organization was actually willing to help him do it, the real shocker is that Kodiak bears were on the list of endangered species.

To grant the wish as efficiently as possible, the Foundation contracted with Safari Club International, which among other things supplied the child with airline tickets and a .340 magnum rifle. The storm of criticism that followed almost forced the Foundation out of business. As the *Times* article put it, "The program that has provided thousands of families with joyful memories to help ease the depression of losing a child is on the hit list of virtually every animal-rights group in the nation."[3]

The members of the Foundation failed to put themselves in the shoes of other stakeholders, empathize with them, or act in ways that would acknowledge, let alone fulfill, their wishes. They failed to see that there is no trade-off between granting the wish of a dying child and the hunting of an animal that was on the endangered species list. While the hunting of endangered species may be on the wish list of a dying child, it cannot be on that of a Foundation. By not considering other alternatives and the implications of their actions, one could argue that the Foundation was the one who behaved like a child.

Flash forward to the present. We are willing to bet (we don't know for sure) that the Humane Society of America was one of the animal rights organizations that so roundly criticized the Make-A-Wish Foundation, and rightly so. For this very reason, what the Humane Society has done recently is every bit as bad, and maybe even worse, than the actions of the Make-A-Wish Foundation.

In August 27, 2007, immediately after Michael Vick, the Atlanta Falcons' star quarterback who pleaded guilty to aiding and abetting dog fights, stepped down from the podium from which he apologized for his heinous acts, a senior member of the Humane Society retrieved the notes that Mr. Vick used in making his apology. Instead of returning them, the Humane Society decided to auction the notes off on eBay so that the profits could be used to protect animals from further abuse.

But it gets even more bizarre. A woman paid $7,400 on eBay for twenty-two Michael Vick football cards that were apparently chewed up and slobbered on by two dogs. The woman admitted that she hadn't even heard of Michael Vick before he was indicted for dog-fighting. The proceeds were also slated to go to the Humane Society.

What Michael Vick did is so bad and so wrong that it defies any understanding or sympathy whatsoever. But how could any organization—especially one that is supposed to uphold our highest ideals and thus serve as a role model—ever justify that it is OK to profit in any way from such despicable and heinous acts?

One explanation is that many organizations that serve the public good get so caught up in themselves and their mission that they

sometimes believe they can do no wrong. Since they are often struggling for money to stay afloat, they are constantly on the edge of
survival. So when an opportunity comes along to serve their cause,
they jump on it. The Humane Society failed to manage the tension
between their serving a commendable cause of helping animals and
their urge to raise more money to do their work more effectively or
perhaps even the urge to restore a sense of justice. Knowing if and
when ends do not justify the means is a sign of emotional maturity
and an ability to take the perspective of others. Making trade-offs
properly, in a mature way, particularly when there are plausible arguments on both sides, is also a sign of moral development.[4] The
Humane Society's actions rank low on all of these scales.

To bring the story up to date, Mr. Vick has since served time and
been released from prison, apologized profusely for his acts, been
reinstated by the National Football League, and been picked up by
the Philadelphia Eagles. But the most significant thing of all is that
he has partnered with the Humane Society to serve as a major fig-
urehead for ending cruelty and violence to animals.

TRIVIAL EVENTS CAN BE EARLY WARNING
SIGNALS OF POTENTIAL CRISES

One could argue that it's petty to pick on the Humane Society because the example of Michael Vick is trivial and therefore not worth
devoting time and space to it. We disagree because whether something is trivial or not depends on how different stakeholders react
to it, and thereby the assumptions one makes. More important,
it ignores the fact that from the standpoint of crisis management
everything is potentially a crisis and should be viewed as such. To
ignore "trivial events" is precisely to ignore potential early warning
signals of more serious crises.

In the past few years, several major environmental organizations such as the Sierra Club and the National Resources Defense
Council have accepted huge amounts of money from big oil and gas
companies with dubious, if not disastrous, environmental records.
In exchange for the money that they need desperately to operate, the

environmental organizations have treaded lightly and toned down considerably their criticisms of the organizations.[5] The Humane Society may be pikers, but the big oil and gas companies are not. Even more to the point, ignoring the seemingly small and trivial cases predisposes one to ignore more important ones.

As Diane Vaughan explained in the context of the *Challenger* disaster (and later on in the context of the *Columbia* disaster), the way managers handle even small and trivial mistakes tells us something about the culture of an organization and the assumptions of its managers.[6] For instance, downplaying the importance of small, trivial events indicates a cultural tendency to consider these events or deviances as "normal." But over time, such deviances will be taken for granted, and hence will redefine the boundaries of values regarding what is normal and what is not, what is risky and what is not, and so on.[7] The theory of the "normalization of deviance" implies that deviations from initial norms and values can slowly reach over time a level that is unacceptable technically, operationally, organizationally, and morally.

Thus, the crises of the Humane Society, the Sierra Club, and the Make-A-Wish Foundation are not only the results of smaller, trivial events that had happened earlier, they are also the early warning signals of even bigger potential crises yet to come.

ASSUMPTIONS

The Make-A-Wish Foundation, the Humane Society, and the Sierra Club are of course just examples of not-for-profit organizations whose basic missions are to do good. Naturally, they are not representative of all such organizations. And of course the examples we have discussed are not representative of everything that they do. Nonetheless, the examples are illuminating precisely because they bring to the surface assumptions that are shared more widely than one would like to believe:

1. Because our basic mission is to do good, we can therefore do no wrong. We certainly cannot commit acts of evil.

2. The outside world thinks like we do; therefore, they will not

only understand but accept what we do. In other words, they will automatically agree with us.

3. The outside world understands that we are constantly struggling to make money so that we can do good; therefore, unless it is patently illegal, they will support all of our efforts to raise money.

4. Because our basic mission is to do good, if we do something, then by definition, it's OK; in other words, we can do things that other kinds of organizations can't even think of doing.

5. To attack us in any way is proof that one is out to destroy us, that is, to do bad.

Of course, we have no exact way of knowing whether each and every one of these assumptions applies precisely to the organizations in question. However, we have conducted enough crisis management audits in not-for-profit organizations to know that unfortunately these same kinds of assumptions do apply to many of them.

But what about for-profit organizations?

Toyota

Most people undoubtedly would have agreed before its safety recalls that Toyota has been more than just a good company: its brand has been one of the finest, its cars of the highest quality, its production system the most reliable, and the company itself one of the most trusted and environmentally friendly. What went wrong?

Toyota's recall crisis began to attract attention when a CHP officer and the members of his family died in a loaner Lexus. The previous driver of the Lexus had complained to the dealership that the car had unintended acceleration problems. Unfortunately, this complaint, an early warning signal of what was to come a few days later, was neither transmitted to the right persons nor addressed properly. Sudden unintended acceleration problems reported by Toyota owners forced the company to issue several large-scale safety recalls later on.

In an early video clip Toyota posted on the Web, a Toyota VP insisted strongly, and somewhat arrogantly, that the problem was the "wrong-sized floor mats" and cited the results of several National Highway Transportation Safety Administration (NHTSA) investigations that had found no vehicle-based defects. And besides the faulty floor mats, he blamed, albeit indirectly but unapologetically, driver error as the main cause of unintended accelerations. This statement made some Toyota owners feel that they had been betrayed by the company, particularly when they found out that the fixes designed to prevent "driver error" did not stop sudden accelerations. Blaming the drivers instead of apologizing to them, loaning out a vehicle without disclosing or fixing its problems, and allowing its VPs to communicate arrogantly provided evidence that Toyota failed to put itself in the shoes of its customers.

Although investigations are under way and thus it is still too early to conclude with certainty that Toyota will be found guilty, evidence suggests that in 2003 Toyota hired an NHTSA employee, who worked later on with his ex-colleagues, to narrow the scope of the investigation of Toyota's problems. There are even allegations by whistleblowers and former employees that high-level Toyota executives tried to cover up the acceleration problems. A recently surfaced internal memo showed that Toyota put profits above safety. In the memo, the Toyota Safety Group bragged about the $100 million they saved on recent recalls.

Toyota's failures are at least partly a direct reflection of its misplaced priorities. Toyota CEO Akio Toyoda said in his testimony to Congress that the three traditional priorities of Toyota, "First, safety; second, quality; third, volume," became confused. It seems that Toyota got caught up in its goal to become the largest car manufacturer in the world, a goal Toyota accomplished in 2008 by outpacing General Motors for the first time in seventy-seven years.[8] In other words, Toyota failed to manage the trade-off between volume, safety, and quality. The goal of being the largest car manufacturer in the world trumped Toyota's other priorities. It is also evidence that Toyota failed to take the perspective of its various stakeholders, including customers, suppliers, and even shareholders.

Toyota's Mega-Crisis

In terms of Chapter 3, it is relatively easy to show how the Make-A-Wish Foundation and the Humane Society both potentially faced mega-crises. For instance, in each case they faced a potentially huge PR crisis brought about by negative publicity. This could have easily morphed into huge economic crises if the public was so turned off that they stopped donating money to both organizations. Thus, in the case of the Humane Society, actions that were designed to raise more money for a financially strapped organization could have potentially ended up costing it even more. In addition, both organizations could have been subject to criminal or psychopathic attacks. For instance, the actions of the Make-A-Wish Foundation could have angered extremist environmentalists so much that they might have been willing to commit acts of violence against it. It could have provoked disgruntled employees to strike back. In this way, one could come up with a virtually unlimited number of plausible scenarios that would cause mega-crises and mega-messes for both organizations.

For Toyota, what started out as a recall has already turned into a mega-crisis. The fiery crash in San Diego and subsequent media attention triggered a chain reaction of other crises: huge worldwide recalls; a significant drop in sales; a significant drop in the market value of the company (more than $20 billion in five months as of June 2010); untold damage to Toyota's reputation; alleged violations of federal law by hiring a former NHTSA employee; alleged cover-ups of sudden acceleration problems; and major lawsuits filed by victims or their families, by Toyota owners who believe that the company has lied to them, and by Toyota shareholders who believe that the company misrepresented the value of the company.

Toyota drivers still do not know for sure what is causing sudden accelerations. Toyota has stopped blaming faulty floor mats and driver error as the only causes of sudden accelerations and has begun to focus on mechanical problems such as sticky gas pedals. But evidence suggests that even after such mechanical fixes, some Toyota vehicles are still suffering from the same problem. Some experts believe that Toyota cannot fix them because it does not know all of the causes of the problem. Others argue, but Toyota denies, that some Toyota vehicles have electronics or software problems.

The issue, however, is no longer about whether Toyota knows how to fix sudden accelerations. Mostly due to poor management, it has become a crisis of trust. To fix the trust issue, Toyota must first admit that there is an electronics and software problem, share its proprietary acceleration and braking system designs with others who can help figure out the problem, and lead the industry (as it has done in the past) to raise and meet its quality standards on electronics and software. The aviation industry standards can be the ideal to reach.

If history is any guide, most of Toyota's problems will be forgotten in a few years, but the challenge for Toyota to avoid similar crises in the future is this: its executives must be willing to apply Toyota's legendary problem-solving skills to Toyota itself, and to see that they need not only a technical redesign of acceleration and braking systems of Toyota vehicles but also a cultural rejuvenation of "The Toyota Way." We will say more on "culture" in the following chapters, but we first want to examine why for-profit organizations often do things that are self-defeating.

WHY FOR-PROFIT ORGANIZATIONS DO INADVISABLE THINGS TO MAKE MORE PROFITS

Whereas not-for-profit organizations seem to suppress everything except that which moves them toward their goals of doing good, some for-profit organizations may repress everything except that which moves them toward the goal of obtaining greater profits, or in more technical terms, greater shareholder value. In fact, the most dominant form of corporate governance today, namely the shareholder value maximization model, is grounded in the principle that the only duty of managers, within legal limits and ethics, is to maximize shareholder value.[9] The shareholder model assumes that because shareholders are the last ones to get their money back if something goes wrong with the company and if there is anything left after paying off creditors, suppliers, and all of the other stakeholders, shareholders are motivated to make sure that managers will utilize company assets and resources efficiently and effectively.[10]

In the context of crises, however, the main premise of shareholder value maximization boils down to something like this: managers should include a stakeholder[11] in an organization's crisis preparations and responses if and only if the stakeholder has or is foreseen to have a significant influence on shareholder value. In effect, the shareholder value maximization model encourages an organization to ignore those stakeholders that are victimized by its actions if they lack the economic power and legal legitimacy to influence an organization's profits negatively.[12]

The principle of the shareholder value maximization model can thus be in conflict with some of our most fundamental prima facie duties.[13] For example, the duty of reparation requires managers to make amends for their wrongful acts even when denial of their role in causing or mismanaging a crisis is in the best interests of shareholders.[14] In the context of crises, the duty of beneficence requires managers to act in a way that benefits not only their shareholders but also their stakeholders. The duty of non-maleficence requires managers not to harm or injure others, both before and after a crisis. Denying any responsibility, being less cooperative, hiding the truth, and shutting off all communications with defenseless stakeholders, even when legally allowed, may further harm or injure these already victimized stakeholders.

To put it differently, the shareholder value maximization model does not encourage managers to put themselves in the shoes of all their stakeholders. In fact, it almost seems to discourage them from doing so if they only try to see things from their shareholders' perspectives. In the shareholder value maximization model, managers are not viewed as moral agents. They are viewed almost as automatons whose only duty is to maximize profits. As a result, the model ignores a fundamental aspect of what makes us human: ethical and moral emotions.[15] Just for this reason alone, the shareholder value maximization model ranks low on moral development and emotional intelligence scales. Our experiences with organizations suggest that it also leads to the following set of deep-seated and damaging assumptions:

1. Because we have a fiduciary duty to maximize profits, we cannot act in a socially responsible way unless such actions also increase profits.

2. The shareholder value maximization model is the most logical and efficient model of corporate governance; it is also supported by the legal system; therefore, society will not only understand and accept what we do, it will automatically agree with us.

3. Society understands that we are constantly struggling to lower cost and increase revenues so that we can maximize shareholder value; therefore, unless what we do is patently illegal, it will support all of our efforts to maximize shareholder wealth.

4. Because our basic mission is to maximize shareholder value, if we accomplish this, then by definition, it's OK; in other words, we can do things that organizations that failed to maximize shareholder wealth can't even think of doing.

5. To attack us in any way is proof that one is out to destroy us, that is, to do bad.

CONCLUDING REMARKS

Not only is it very difficult to accept that good organizations are just as capable of doing unwise and bad things as any of us, we are stunned when they do it. It violates one of our deepest-held assumptions: because good people and good organizations are "good," they are therefore exempt from doing bad things. The more that bad organizations do bad things, the more we want to believe that there is a set of organizations that are incapable of doing bad.

We have drawn from various disciplines such as emotional intelligence, sociology of disasters, corporate governance, and moral development to understand why good organizations do bad things. Our discussion has led us to the following conclusions.

First of all, no organization is exempt from crises. And good organizations such as Make-A-Wish Foundation, the Humane Society, and Toyota are just as capable of doing immature, unwise, or child-ish things as any other organizations.

Second, a part of what causes good organizations and their managers to do bad things is their low levels of emotional intelligence: they cannot manage effectively their moral emotions and conflicts or trade-offs, and they cannot empathize with a large variety of stakeholders. Simply put, they behave immaturely.

Third, if such immature behaviors have not already caused a crisis, they are early warning signals of potentially more serious ones. For instance, Vaughan's theory of normalization implies that ignoring seemingly small and trivial deviations from original norms and values, if repeated over and over again, leads to the acceptance of such deviations as normal. As a result, managers not only end up engaging in more and more deviant behavior, they also start believing that their assumptions about the world and their stakeholders are true. Deviant behaviors and wrong assumptions become the norm, the expected, taken for granted. Thus immature behavior should not be dismissed as trivial and excused. It should be taken as an opportunity to learn about how organizations get themselves into trouble—that is, crises.

The moral is that especially in today's world, the only protection one has is "know thy assumptions." Every organization, whether for-profit or not-for profit, needs to know and to track its key assumptions over time.

Fourth, the dominant form of corporate governance, the shareholder value maximization model, seems to promote immature behavior by for-profit organizations. It does so by failing to view managers as moral agents. In other words, it reduces managers to a subset of what they really are and encourages them to treat their stakeholders in the same way: only as means and not also ends in themselves.

In the next chapter, we will begin to analyze how the culture of an industry brought the global financial system to the brink of collapse.

Corporation, n. An ingenious device for obtaining individual profit without individual responsibility.

—AMBROSE BIERCE, *The Devil's Dictionary*

[O]ut of the particular culture, strategy, and worldview of investment banks arises [their] compensation structure—when mixed with job insecurity—[it] creates (and is created by) a "bubble culture" of expediency, an approach to people and to corporations (including themselves and their own companies) that is based on generating quick, short-term rewards. [In other words, Wall Street not only sold highly risky investments to others, but to itself as well. In more prosaic terms, it bought its own junk!] . . . In such a practice of squeezing the most out of the present, the end (the bursting of the bubble [that is, a mega-crisis])—is not only presumed and often expected, but also made possible. In many cases, Wall Streeters expect that their behavior toward corporations, even governments, will in time result in busts. . . . Moreover, many of my informants anticipated not only a crash, but also an *eventual bailout*, on the grounds that Wall Street investment banks were "too big to fail." Such an assumption demonstrates that, contrary to their free market discourses, investment banks embraced risk not because they had successfully hedged their bets or managed their exposure. Rather, they depend on the state [government] and the global interconnectedness of the economy to absorb the risk while they focus on immediate profits.

—KAREN HO, *Liquidated*

T HE PRECEDING CHAPTER looked at a set of dubious assumptions that lie on the relative surface of organizations. That is, one does not necessarily have to be a member of the organizations in order to be able to see the assumptions.

This chapter digs deeper. It looks at the assumptions that constitute the deepest inner core, the culture, of organizations. By definition, these assumptions are not easily visible to those outside of an organization or industry. And, in fact, because they are taken for granted, they are often invisible to those on the inside as well. In other words, they are the "shadow" of an organization. As a result, they are largely unconscious. They rush to the defense of an organization when it needs to protect itself from real and imagined threats.

Although the examples in this chapter are drawn primarily from the finance industry, with little modification they apply to virtually all industries. For this reason alone, they are important to examine and to critique.

The chapter also identifies a set of beliefs and assumptions that the finance industry needs to internalize if it wants to become a trust-enhancing culture. It concludes with a set of rationalizations that in principle apply to all organizations, and for which they need to be on guard lest they make them susceptible to crises.

THE DARK SIDE OF WALL STREET:
HOW THE MIND-SET OF THE FINANCIAL
INDUSTRY GOT US INTO A MESS

Over the months in which the financial crisis unfolded, Mitroff has had repeated conversations with a friend who works for a major bank. To protect his identity, we'll call him Adam Smith (obviously not his real name).

Adam has uncovered some of the primary assumptions and beliefs that drive the financial industry. The assumptions and beliefs
that he has exposed result from hours of interviews and conversations that Adam has conducted with some of the top analysts,
managers, and executives of some of this country's key financial
institutions. They are also the result of his analyzing countless
books, reports, and articles. They derive as well from his many
hours of working among and thus observing at first hand the behavior of the "natives."

As we noted in earlier chapters, the complexity of the financial
instruments involved and the lack of proper regulation of the industry are certainly key factors in understanding what got us into
the current financial crisis. Nonetheless, the primary focus of Adam
and the authors has been on the general mind-set of those at the
top of the finance industry and the culture of risk they promote and
reward.[1] Various studies establish that a leader's perception of risk
is one of the underlying causes of a crisis.[2] The cues that leaders
transmit do not have to be clear to change the perceptions of risk
within an organization or industry. Subtle cues are often sufficient.[3]
Thus, unless we change the mind-set and culture within financial
organizations, merely altering or regulating external factors alone
won't prevent future catastrophes.[4] Indeed, if the history of past
financial crises is any guide, once things return to normal, the old
habits of mind will return as well.[5]

As unwritten rules of the game, the *individual* assumptions and
beliefs we have identified are rarely stated.[6] They are certainly not
written down in formal documents. If you have to ask what they
are, then you're not "part of the club." In contrast, the *total system* of these interrelated beliefs and assumptions virtually is never
stated at all.[7] But without seeing them as a whole, it is impossible
to see how they are interconnected and reinforce one another. Most
damning of all, seeing them as a whole reveals that the industry
not only permits but rewards primitive behavior.[8] In short, the assumptions identified in the list below are the hidden, dark side of
Wall Street.[9]

Of course it goes without saying that not everyone in the industry subscribes to these and other dubious beliefs, and certainly not all to the same degree. Nonetheless, all of Adam's experience and ours points to the fact that when things are going well, an overwhelming majority not only overlooks the unspoken rules but tolerates them quite well:

1. We are the Masters of the Universe; when required we can manipulate anything and anybody to our advantage; we can "game the numbers and the system to serve our needs."

2. We're smarter than anyone else; in fact, we're the smartest guys in any room (shades of Enron![10]). Unless you are as smart as us, you can't possibly understand the complicated financial instruments we've invented. You certainly can't understand what we do. If we can't understand them, then no one can.

3. We don't need controls and regulations, certainly not by others. We have been selected for our unique skills and talents. We have worked harder than anyone else to get where we are today. As a result, we know what's best for us.

4. We bet and play with others' money. It's a high-risk, high-reward environment. It's not for everyone.

5. While other people matter to a certain extent, we matter more because we're the ones in charge and in the driver's seat. We are entitled to the huge amounts of money we make because of the value of the huge deals that we bring to market.

6. We don't fail, period! We're too big and important to fail. Indeed, the world cannot allow us to fail because we are essential to the functioning of the world's capital markets.

7. Since numbers are the only things that really matter, we can manage risk by reducing it to a mathematical equation.

8. You are only as good as your "last kill," that is, "big deal." If you are not producing, then you are not valued.

9. To succeed you have to make difficult decisions. And, to make

the best decisions, emotions have to be put aside. There is no room for bleeding hearts. If in order to get ahead you have to fire your best friend, then don't think twice about doing it; if you don't do it, then you're a p***y and a wimp!

10. We can't control the markets. We just pay attention to today and to the transactions immediately in front of us that are within our control.

11. If you're standing still, then you're "moving backward." Always keep moving ahead.

12. We are a culture based on performance. We are constantly grading and weeding out the weak and underperforming.

One cannot help but wonder what the results would be if someone who acted in accord with all of these twelve assumptions took the Minnesota Multiphasic Personality Inventory (MMPI), a psychological test that is used to identify various psychopathologies. What would the correlation be between the behaviors of those who subscribed to nearly all of the preceding assumptions and various psychopathologies? We bet it would be high.[11]

All of the assumptions and beliefs are a direct reflection of the narrow-mindedness and insularity of the industry. They are not only an expression of a deep sense of entitlement, they reinforce it. They are a reflection of the narcissism that is characteristic of so much of today's business world, and society in general.

Following is a list of traits or patterns the *Diagnostic and Statistical Manual of Mental Disorders* of the American Psychological Association, 4th ed., identifies as narcissistic. If a person exhibits five of the following behaviors, he or she is considered to have a narcissistic personality disorder:[12]

1. Has a grandiose sense of self-importance (e.g., exaggerates achievements and talents, expects to be recognized as superior without commensurate achievements)

2. Is preoccupied with fantasies of unlimited success, power, brilliance, beauty, or ideal love

3. Believes he or she is "special" and unique and can only be understood by, or should associate with, other special or high-status people (or institutions)

4. Requires excessive admiration

5. Has a sense of entitlement, i.e., unreasonable expectations of especially favorable treatment or automatic compliance with his or her expectations

6. Is interpersonally exploitative, i.e., takes advantage of others to achieve his or her own ends

7. Lacks empathy: is unwilling to recognize or identify with the feelings and needs of others

8. Is often envious of others or believes that others are envious of him or her

9. Shows arrogant, haughty behaviors or attitudes

If they were acknowledged, then those aspects of the culture of Wall Street that both attract and promote narcissistic behavior could be addressed. Unfortunately, this is not likely to occur soon.

One of the things that Adam and the authors find most distressing is the fact that if one even tried to raise these beliefs for analysis and discussion with the members of the finance industry, one would immediately be dismissed for bringing up something that has no relevance whatsoever to the world of finance. The authors know this not only from their years of personal consulting but from years of teaching MBAs as well.

The many times when the authors have tried to initiate discussions of these and other assumptions and beliefs with students in their MBA classes, a sizable number, mostly finance majors, were outright hostile and attempted to disrupt the proceedings. It was literally impossible to have a discussion, let alone to engage in an analysis. This was the case no matter how mildly the assumptions and beliefs were stated. Any discussion was basically just too threatening.

There is no way around the fact that the preceding assumptions and beliefs constitute a self-sealing and self-perpetuating system. In other words, they serve as strong defense mechanisms.

ASSUMPTIONS AND BELIEFS AS
DEFENSE MECHANISMS

Assumptions and beliefs are rarely recognized as defense mechanisms. That is one of the primary reasons why they are so difficult to acknowledge, let alone change.

Table 5.1 shows a set of beliefs and assumptions that are prevalent on Wall Street. Each assumption or belief is an example of various types of Freudian defense mechanisms.[13]

The first column of the table gives the traditional form of a particular defense mechanism as it was first discovered and formulated by Freud and others. The defense mechanisms manifest themselves in the assumptions or beliefs shown in the second column. The third column provides examples of the defense mechanisms that have been used by Wall Street as well as other organizations.

THE SHADOW

A discussion of defense mechanisms would not be complete without an understanding of the concept of the "shadow." According to Jung, the "shadow" includes everything a person "refuses to acknowledge about himself and yet is always thrusting upon him, for instance inferior traits of character and other incompatible tendencies."[14] The concept of the "shadow" at the level of an industry can be understood as a set of facts it "wishes to deny due to the threat they pose to its self-image and self-understanding and, more generally, the need to be viewed in a favorable light by others."[15] Acknowledging, accepting, and coming to terms with one's shadow, whether at the individual, organizational, or industrial level, helps one accomplish two important goals: honest and accurate recognition of oneself, and open and truthful communication with others.[16]

Of what has the financial industry, or Wall Street, been in denial? Table 5.1 helps us to understand a few of the repressed traits

TABLE 5.1. Freudian defense mechanisms

Defense mechanism	Assumption or belief	Example
Intellectualization	"The probabilities of anything bad happening are small."	Long-Term Capital Management collapsed as the result of a low-probability event that was ignored in their models.[1]
Disavowal	"Impacts are small and therefore negligible."	Many people agreed with Bernanke when he said in March 2007 to the Congress's Joint Economic Committee that "the impact on the broader economy and financial markets of the problems in the subprime markets seems likely to be contained."[2]
Grandiosity	"We're so big and powerful that nothing bad can happen to us."	Several large companies believed that they would survive because they are "too big to fail."[3]
Compartmentalization	"Bad things can't affect the whole system. That is, things are contained, limited, and separable."	A small London branch office (with a dozen or so staff) was not paid too much attention until it brought down AIG, the largest insurer in the world.[4]
Projection	"Someone else is to blame."	AIG blamed the "perfect financial storm" for its woes.[5]
Idealization	"We don't have problems.	Before the financial crisis, Wall Street was extremely confident that its risk management models worked well.[6]
Rationalization	"It won't happen to us."	Wall Street believes that our economy is the largest and the most dynamic in the world. ·Our goldilocks economy is a reflection of all the lessons we learned from past crises. We will never experience again something like the Great Depression.

1. Roger Lowerstein, *When Genius Failed: The Rise and Fall of Long-Term Capital Management* (New York: Random House Trade Paperbacks, 2001).

2. Associated Press, "Mortgage Problems Aren't Spreading to Economy," March 28, 2007, http://www.startribune.com/business/11216636.html?elr=KArksUUUoDEy3LGDiO7aiU (accessed August 3, 2010).

3. Karen Ho, *Liquidated: An Ethnography of Wall Street* (Durham, NC: Duke University Press, 2009), 291.

4. Peter Koeing, "AIG Trail Leads to London Casino," *London Telegraph*, October 18, 2008.

5. Al Bawaba, "AIG Blames 'Perfect Financial Storm' for Its Woes," *ProQuest, ABI/INFORM Trade & Industry*, doc. ID: 1819062511, August 6, 2009.

6. Emily Thornton, "Inside Wall Street's Culture of Risk," *Bloomberg Business Week*, June 12, 2006, http://www.businessweek.com/magazine/content/06_24/b3988004.htm (accessed August 3, 2010).

or issues. It is not an exaggeration to say that its highly sophisticated financial tools are not sophisticated enough or that they are too complex to understand even for industry members; industry members' assumptions and models about how the world works are flawed; members cannot account for black swan events; they are embarrassed to receive taxpayers' money; they could not see the downturn coming; they knew that the crisis was coming but they didn't care; and, finally, they are neither the best and the brightest nor the most responsible and trustworthy. For if they were, they might not have experienced the problems above.

Wall Street has a difficult task ahead. Solving the problems in the financial system requires that Wall Street understand and accept how it has evolved into its current, seemingly unsustainable form and has contributed to the financial crisis. In other words, Wall Street must confront its shadow. Ossified and rigid defense mechanisms, assumptions, and outdated beliefs are among the biggest obstacles for anyone trying to confront one's shadow. But becoming a more responsible contributor to society means that all individuals, organizations, and industries have to accept ownership for their problems, stop rationalizing their way out of them, and stop projecting them onto others.

A CULTURE OF TRUST

History shows that financial systems based on the set of dubious assumptions and erroneous beliefs discussed in this chapter are not sustainable in the long term.[17] A financial system is basically a trust-based system. No financial system can operate effectively without it.

Even after the financial crisis, society still has to assume that the financial system is trustworthy. For instance, we still trust "money" in that we believe that it is a valid form of payment and assume that others do as well. We want to trust the banks. We want to believe they will be there tomorrow so that we can get our savings back. We want to believe once again that our pension funds, insurance companies, and investment advisors have our best interests at heart. We want to trust regulators and policymakers. For example, the phrases "Greenspan put" or "Bernanke put," which refer to the Federal Reserve chairman's monetary policy of lowering the Federal Funds interest rate to combat a possible crisis, reflect our trust in the ability of the Fed, "the lender of last resort," and its chairman to "insure" the health of the financial system and the economy. In short, trust is an integral part of any financial system.

For this reason, it is understandable that many people were outraged when they realized how Wall Street abused their trust by cultivating a culture that put the sustainability of the whole financial system at risk, and yet was bailed out by taxpayers' money. It is therefore incumbent upon us to offer a set of rules or beliefs, however limited, that a trust-enhancing culture would have:

1. We are the Moral Masters of the Universe; we never manipulate anything and anybody to our advantage; although we have the power to "game the numbers and the system to serve our needs," we just don't.

2. Although we can regulate ourselves, but because no one is perfect, we also need external controls and regulations as well.

3. We never bet and play with your money. We don't take risks with your money, even those that we take with ours.

4. We are entitled to the amounts of money we make only to the extent that we bring value to the market and do so responsibly.

5. We make mistakes, and we fail! But we never want to be too big and important to fail. In fact, we do not want to let the world down because we are essential to the functioning of the world's capital markets.

6. Since moral values are the only things that really matter, we manage risk by never reducing it solely to a mathematical equation.

7. We are only as moral as our last actions. If we are not acting morally, then we ought not to be valued.

8. To succeed we have to make difficult decisions. And to make the best decisions, our values and emotions, as well as those

of others, must never be put aside. There is no room for machismo.

9. We can't control the markets. But to protect your interests, we do our best to pay attention to the future.

10. We are a culture based on trust. We are constantly grading and weeding out the untrustworthy.

Idealistic? Without a doubt. The point is that the gap between the two sets of cultural norms presented in this chapter shows how wide the chasm is between where we are currently and where we need (ought) to be ethically. For this reason, we want to give an example of how a culture based on trust would have approached the messy issue of the risk associated with financial derivatives:

Derivatives are useful in many ways but they are also risky because we don't understand them completely. The regulators don't either. For example, credit default swap (CDS) contracts are considered a type of insurance but they are not regulated like insurance contracts; there is no oversight, there is no transparency, there are no leverage limits in the CDS market. The system as a whole is unsustainable in the long term. True, some of us will make a lot of money in the short term by taking advantage of the fact that no one really understands the long-term effects of financial derivatives. But most of us won't; for it is not the right thing to do. Doing so also undermines the society's trust in the financial system. In fact, as soon as we identify those who take advantage of the weaknesses in the financial system, we try to stop them. We also collaborate with regulatory agencies to design regulatory frameworks to make the financial system as sustainable and trustworthy as possible. We owe this to everyone.

CONCLUDING REMARKS

We ignore assumptions at our own peril and that of others. The Socratic dictum to "know thyself" applies as much, and perhaps even more, to organizations as it does to individuals. Knowing one's self or culture sometimes requires one to confront one's beliefs and assumptions as well as one's dark side or shadow. But that requires an immense amount of emotional pain and effort because of the defense mechanisms one employs to protect one's self. The process of getting to know one's self and confronting one's shadow is messy and scary. In fact, if managed poorly, it can turn into a crisis. This is why most people and organizations resist engaging in it. But not engaging in it leads to even bigger crises.

Previous research has established that organizations that are prone to crises endorse and use defense mechanisms such as denial, rationalization, and so on significantly more than organizations that are not prone to crises.[18] These organizations are not only less prepared for crises, they also deny that they need to receive crisis management training and need to have robust crisis management plans and procedures.[19]

The list below presents a brief sample of the many kinds of rationalizations that the authors have encountered as to why an organization (or industry) believes that it will not have a crisis and therefore why it is exempt from the need to have an effective program of crisis management.[20] How one can deal with defense mechanisms is the topic of the next chapter.

> *Dangerous Rationalizations*
> Our size will protect us.
> Excellent companies don't have crises.
> Our location will protect us.
> Certain crises only happen to others.
> If a crisis happens, someone will rescue us.
> Crisis management is someone else's responsibility.
> Each crisis is so unique that it is pointless to prepare.

PART II

MANAGING
ASSUMPTIONS

6   OVERCOMING MEGA-DENIAL

In October 1983, six months after becoming CEO of Corning Inc . . . [Jamie] Houghton called his first meeting of the company's top 150 executives from around the world. Convinced that the company was in deep trouble, Houghton was determined to set a tone decidedly different from the convivial gatherings of the past.

"So my opening speech was not polite," he says. "I pointed out that our financial results were appalling, the organizational morale worse, and that as organizational leaders we were disgraceful. I said that our first task was to admit that we were at the bottom and had nowhere to go but up." After comparing the company to an alcoholic who must first admit to the seriousness of his problem before having any chance of recovery, Houghton walked off the stage to dead silence.

—DAVID NADLER, *Champions of Change*

IN CHAPTER 5, we argued that the immature behavior that organizations often exhibit is a consequence of the beliefs and assumptions deeply ingrained in their culture. Furthermore, immaturity is not just a temporary phase but a permanent property of the culture.

In this chapter, we argue that, depending on their levels of maturity and development (moral, emotional, cognitive, or spiritual), managers and organizations not only define crises, mega-crises, messes, and mega-messes differently, they view, experience, and manage them differently.

At the highest levels, crises and messes are accepted as fundamental aspects of the universe. And they are managed as such.

At the lowest levels, mega-crises and mega-messes generate enormous anxiety. They cause unconscious fears and anxieties to bubble up from the past and trigger the kinds of defense mechanisms that were discussed in the previous chapter. Such fears and anxieties cannot be easily dismissed or treated by ordinary and primarily "rational" means. Even the most rational and plausible arguments will often fail to convince those who have deep fears and feelings about messy situations and crises. These fears and anxieties need to be faced and treated by methods that derive from psychodynamics.

We discuss briefly several general strategies for overcoming denial, fear, and resistance. These strategies also help managers and organizations advance along multiple developmental lines.

MEGA-CRISES AND MEGA-MESSES GENERATE MEGA-ANXIETY AND MEGA-DENIAL

It is putting it mildly to say that mega-crises generate enormous anxiety. Because mega-crises have the potential to wreak enormous destruction, the possibility of their leaving physical and emotional scars that can last for years, if not for a lifetime, is huge.[1]

Similarly, even though not all mega-messes necessarily become mega-crises, they are capable of generating enormous anxiety as well. They certainly have the potential to generate intense feelings of being overwhelmed and of helplessness.

If actually experiencing mega-crises and mega-messes wasn't bad enough, often just thinking about the possibility of their occurring is enough to produce feelings of anxiety. For this reason alone, it is not surprising that mega-crises produce mega-denial.[2] In fact, it may be argued that the bigger the magnitude of a crisis, the lower the chances of its happening, or both, the stronger the denial. Many people, organizations, and societies prefer not to think about mega-crises and mega-messes, and believe that if we don't think about them they will somehow magically go away. But, as we have argued throughout, not thinking about and not preparing for mega-crises is not an option. It only makes them worse. Evidence establishes that when managers, groups, and organizations are faced with a threatening situation such as a crisis, they hamper how they process information, become more controlling, centralize decision making, and increase pressure toward uniformity.[3] Simply put, they behave rigidly; if the situation is too threatening, they may even freeze up.[4]

Behaving rigidly or freezing up, of course, is exactly the opposite of what managers and organizations must do to cope with a threatening situation, whether it is a mess or a full-blown crisis. For the reasons mentioned, managers fail to respond effectively to a crisis, particularly in the heat of the crisis. Evidence also suggests that to avoid behaving rigidly, managers and organizations must have practiced how to respond to a crisis before it occurs. Effective crisis preparations, training, and simulations repeatedly have been shown to help managers cope with crises.[5]

In fact, scientific evidence that has been accumulated over many years shows that preparing for crises leads to successful outcomes.

THE LITERATURE
The literature on crises and crisis management lends strong support to the following findings and propositions:

- The number and frequency of crises has been increasing exponentially in the past several decades and particularly since the 1970s.[6]
- While the total costs of crises are difficult to measure and to predict empirically, nevertheless, there are estimates of the economic costs of crises: Three Mile Island Nuclear Power Plant crisis ($4 billion);[7] Johnson & Johnson's Tylenol crisis ($500 million);[8] Union Carbide explosion in Bhopal, India (between $500 million and $1 billion, plus a takeover attack);[9]

Enron's collapse (bankruptcy of two large organizations and more than $60 billion);[10] WorldCom's bankruptcy (around $116 billion write-offs in assets and debt);[11] September 11 terrorist attacks ($2 trillion);[12] the global financial crisis ($4.1 trillion).[13] One of the very few empirical studies reported that 25 percent of those organizations that experience a crisis do not survive. Furthermore, the direct costs of crises are on the order of tens of millions of dollars.[14] Unfortunately, the social and emotional costs of crises largely remain incalculable and are not included.

- A previous study by the authors found that for every *two* crises that crisis-prepared organizations experienced in a year, crisis-prone organizations experienced *three*.[15] Moreover, when crisis-prepared organizations experienced a crisis, they recovered substantially faster.[16] The same studies also suggested that crisis-prone organizations are significantly less profitable; for example, the profitability of crisis-prone companies (4 percent average of return on assets for three years) was significantly lower than the profitability of crisis-prepared companies (6 percent) during the same period.[17]

- The economic costs of being prepared for major crises (the best estimates are 1.5 percent of lost income) pale in comparison to the total costs of managing a crisis. In short, any business strategy that doesn't incorporate crisis preparedness is not strategic at all; in fact, strategic management and crisis management are flip sides of the same coin.[18]

- Crises threaten large sets of stakeholders; not only do they directly harm organizations, their consumers, employees, and nearby communities, but the impacts of crises can reach beyond geographic boundaries (for example, Chernobyl). They have the potential to victimize even more remote stakeholders, such as future generations.[19]

- Traditional models of corporate governance—with their emphasis on contracts, cost-benefit analyses, and preparing only for higher probability or "normal" crises—are at best inadequate and at worst fail miserably and ethically in the context of crises.[20]

• Crisis preparedness (prevention, containment, resilience, and so on) is generally successful; therefore, it should be a high-priority item on the agenda of all organizations.[21] In other words, crisis management and preparedness (prevention, containment, resilience) is not only an economic imperative, it is also an ethical one.

Given the preceding, we conclude that there are *no good rational or ethical reasons* for being *un*prepared for major crises. However, the fact that strong evidence and compelling arguments often fail to convince a significant number of organizations that they should have robust programs of crisis management shows that something other than self-interest or rationality is at work, namely, emotional denial and resistance.

The upshot is that all the so-called "rational" data and moral arguments in the world will not convince someone who has deep emotional fears and feelings to undertake crisis management for his or her organization. Thus the fundamental problem in getting organizations to adopt crisis management is overcoming fear, denial, and resistance. Interestingly, overcoming fear, denial, and resistance is also key to managing messes and crises effectively.

Then, what can managers and organizations do to overcome these strong feelings?

SEVEN STRATEGIES FOR OVERCOMING FEAR, DENIAL, AND RESISTANCE

There are several general strategies for overcoming fear, denial, and resistance. Our intent is not to discuss each in detail, but rather to spell out in broad outlines the nature of each so that the reader has an overall picture of the various options that are available. The interested reader is referred to the sources in the endnotes for further details.

It is important to note that none of the strategies that we outline will work perfectly for all organizations. Indeed, there are certain types of organizations for which nothing seems to work. Some
organizations are so crisis prone that transforming them is virtually
impossible. The trouble is that crisis-prone organizations pose a serious threat not only to themselves but to the larger environment
as well. If only for this reason, we need to discover new methods to
help all organizations to become better prepared for crises.[22]

Seven strategies are listed below. First of all, none are sufficient
in and of themselves. Second, using one of them does not preclude
using any of the others and at the same time. In other words, the
methods and strategies are neither exclusive nor exhaustive. Third,
because some of them (such as coaching) are much better known
than others, we do not devote equal space to each of them. We focus
on the lesser-known ones so as to serve readers better by expanding
their toolkits. Fourth, the methods and strategies generally differ in
the "depth" to which they "penetrate" to locate problems within the
psyches of individuals and organizations. Some methods are closer to
the surface in that they treat the presenting symptoms of problems,
while others necessitate probing deep beneath the surface to locate
the underlying causes within the unconscious of individuals and of
organizations. The basic premise of all methods of psychodynamics
is that the kinds of crises that a person experienced early in his or her
life are strong determinants of how a person can and will respond to
crises later in life.

The seven methods and strategies are

1. Individual and group coaching

2. Individual psychotherapy

3. Group therapy

4. Radical organizational change

5. Organizational therapy

6. Individual transformation or spirituality

7. Organizational transformation or spirituality

Individual and Group Coaching
Coaching has been widely embraced by organizations of all kinds.[23]
In fact, it is a multimillion-dollar-a-year industry.

As a general rule, coaching is not psychotherapy.[24] Even though
many coaches have extensive backgrounds and training in psychology
and psychotherapy, and thus employ them regularly in their work,
the vast majority of coaches tend to focus on the here and now and
not on the past sources of current problems.[25] To be sure, many
coaches focus on how the inevitable conflicts one had in growing
up (such as sibling rivalry) and in past jobs bear on the conflicts one
has in the present. Nonetheless, the primary focus is still on helping
senior executives and managers deal with the conflicts they are currently experiencing with their peers, superiors, and subordinates.[26]

Coaches can be invaluable in helping people negotiate the inevitable conflicts that arise with respect to which kinds of crises occur
and to what extent their organizations should prepare for them. For
instance, coaches can help in identifying the kinds of styles of negotiation that work best with various types of people. Most of all,
they can provide protective and supportive environments in which
one can role-play and practice how someone can interact with different kinds of people in preparing for crises before they happen,
act effectively during the occurrence of a crisis, and debrief without
blaming after a crisis has occurred.

If the conflicts cannot be resolved by methods that are "close to
the surface," then deeper interventions are called for. For example,
if someone experiences frequent panic attacks and recurring night-
mares that affect his or her ability to think about and to work on
difficult issues such as mega-messes and mega-crises, then more intensive interventions may be called for, such as psychotherapy that
deals with issues that are buried deep in one's unconscious. Whatever the case, coaches can be extremely helpful in helping individuals
and organizations decide what forms of intervention are appropriate
for which types of problems. They can even be helpful in suggesting
whether therapy is appropriate, and if so, which kind.

Individual Psychotherapy

Individual psychotherapy is typically recommended if merely con-
templating the possibility of mega-crises and mega-messes triggers
intense and painful memories of past crises that a person has experienced in his or her personal life. For example, if a person has
experienced serious traumas such as physical or sexual abuse, then
individual psychotherapy can be helpful (if not a dire necessity) in
overcoming the distress associated with past events. In assessing
whether individual psychotherapy is recommended, or necessary
or not, and if it is, how extensive it needs to be, a psychologist or
therapist gauges the seriousness of past abuse by determining how
frequently it occurred, how old the person was when it began, who
the abuser was and his or her relationship to the abused (for example, a parent, sibling, relative), how long the abuse lasted, and who
if anyone was complicit in the abuse, such as a parent or sibling.
All of these factors influence whether and how someone responds to
present crises. In other words, the basic premise of psychotherapy
is that the kinds of crises that a person experienced early in life are
strong determinants of how the individual can and will respond to
crises later in life.[27]

Individual psychotherapy is also strongly recommended if unresolved, and hence largely unconscious, conflicts from early in life
affect one's ability to function in the present, for instance, to hold
jobs, maintain healthy relationships with others, and so on—in
short, anything that seriously affects one's ability to function and
to handle life's inevitable conflicts and disappointments.[28]

Needless to say, if one suffers from more serious problems such
as extreme fears, free-floating anxiety, persistent thoughts of suicide, and long-term depression, then individual psychotherapy is not
merely "recommended," it is an absolute necessity.

Group Therapy

Individuals also often can benefit greatly from sharing their problems
in group settings with others who have experienced similar problems
and hence are likely to be both sympathetic and supportive. Even

though many could benefit, group therapy is not as common in organizations. In *The Leader on the Couch: A Clinical Approach to Changing People and Organizations*,[29] the distinguished organizational psychologist and psychotherapist Manfred Kets de Vries presents a number of techniques for overcoming fear, resistance, and denial in organizational settings. One of the most powerful is a week-long series of workshops in which diverse groups of executives from a wide array of industries agree one at a time to put themselves voluntarily in the proverbial hot seat so that they can understand better how unresolved past issues affect their current behavior and decisions.

It is of course one thing to open up in front of a group of executives that one may never see again. It is quite another to transfer the knowledge that one has learned to the settings in which one works, and to open up in front of those with whom one interacts on a frequent basis. For this reason, a critical part of the process is a periodic set of "check-ins" to see "how things are working out back home." In other words, the process is not a one-shot deal but a continually ongoing process.[30]

Radical Organizational Change

Extreme crises offer organizations the rare opportunity to make radical changes. If a crisis, or better yet a series of crises, poses a clear and unmistakable threat to a business, then given the presence of a strong leader or leaders, the organization may have no alternative but to make radical changes in its culture, structure, and mission. The key phrase is "given the presence of a strong leader." Without the persistent efforts of a strong and determined leader or leaders, then radical change is highly unlikely.[31]

Note that rarely can a single leader make radical changes solely by him- or herself. The leader not only has to articulate a new vision but also make it so compelling that he or she gets the "buy in" of significant numbers of the organization. The leader also has to be clear and firm that those who are unable to go along with change have no future with the organization.

Those special leaders who can embrace radical change are the closest that one can find to exemplary models for managing mega-messes and mega-crises. But make no mistake about it; making radical change in any organization means that one first has to understand as much as possible the many factors that influence an organization both within and outside of its usual boundaries. One needs to understand the current mess in which an organization is embedded in order to understand better what needs to change and why. In other words, one needs to understand the whole system in which an organization exists and functions.

Organizational Therapy

Organizational therapy is not the same as group therapy. While organizational therapy obviously draws a great deal from individual and group psychotherapy, the primary "client" is no longer just individuals but the organization as a whole.[32] To be sure, organizational therapy works with specific individuals who are the ones who are most affected and affect the organization and its problems. But it also works with how the structure, reward systems, communication channels, and especially the corporate culture (see Chapter 5) contribute both consciously and unconsciously to the organization's current problems. As we have discussed before, organizations are prone to dysfunctional ego defenses such as denial, rationalization, and projection as much as their individual members.[33]

One of the most important forms of organizational therapy derives from the work of one of the earliest pioneers of psychoanalysis, Melanie Klein.[34] Klein identified one of the key mechanisms by which individuals protect themselves from threatening events and environments: splitting.

Splitting is most easily seen in early childhood when young children typically "split" their mothers into two diametrically opposing parts or opposites: the "good mother," who literally provides nourishment to the helpless child, and the "bad mother," who cannot always meet the child's needs on demand. In fairy tales, which are the archetypal models for representing the psychic conflicts children experience between good and bad mothers, the good mother is typically represented as "the good fairy or godmother" or "the kind witch," whereas the bad mother is typically the "evil witch" or "evil queen." One of the primary reasons why fairy tales appeal to people of all ages is that they represent the unconscious conflicts that all children experience in a form that their young minds can handle. Fairy tales express in stories and symbols what young children cannot say in words. They thus serve as a form of therapy to help young children deal with—literally heal—the "splits" within themselves.

Fairy tales serve another highly important function. Through the resolution of the stories (happy endings), they help the young child to learn that the "good mother" and the "bad mother" are one and the same person. In this way, not only are the split images integrated into a single, real, live human being, but in the process, the child matures as a result.

Nevertheless, the process of splitting does not vanish altogether. Splitting is constantly available to help all of us deal with stressful situations such as a bad boss, rude strangers, politicians, and so on—in short, anyone that arouses strong feelings and deep emotions inside us.

In organizations, splitting typically takes the form of scapegoating. Those who support us are seen as "the good guys" and those who oppose us are naturally seen as "the bad guys."[35] The job of an organizational therapist is to help us to see that "the good and bad guys" are both due partly to our instinctual need to divide the world by projecting the "bad parts of ourselves" that we don't like, and hence repress, onto others. In brief, we overidealize the parts of ourselves that we like and we overly reject the parts we don't like by projecting them onto others. In this way, we often demonize others. This is especially the case when others force us to confront complex, dangerous, painful, and highly threatening situations such as mega-crises.

In short, by establishing deep trust between him or her and the members of an organization, the job of the organizational therapist is to very gently and very patiently help the members to get beyond the need to scapegoat so that they can turn their energies into confronting the real problems they face.

Individual and Organizational Transformation or Spirituality

Although they are not completely identical, individual and organizational transformation or spirituality are close enough that we will discuss them as if they were one.

Of all the topics in this book, this is undoubtedly the most controversial, and perhaps the most difficult to discuss. And yet, for this very reason, it is also potentially the most important and relevant topic of all. It certainly opens up as no other topic can very different definitions and meanings of key terms such as *crisis* and *crisis management.*

The easiest and the most direct way to approach a topic that is fraught with all kinds of enormous conceptual and philosophical difficulties is to state at the outset that virtually all forms of individual and organizational transformation recognize, or postulate if one prefers, that there are various "fundamental stages" of human development that can be clearly differentiated from one another. Furthermore, the various stages form a clear progression from lower to higher. This progression takes place along many lines of development. Table 6.1 shows an example.[36]

The main point of Table 6.1 is that depending on how high or low they rank on different lines of development (moral, emotional, cognitive, spiritual, and so on), managers and organizations will define crises, mega-crises, messes, and mega-messes differently. More important, they will hold a different set of assumptions, follow a different set of moral codes, and implement a different set of crisis management strategies.

For instance, Hawkins illustrates how one views differently another person's crisis, in this case, a "bum" or homeless person, depending on where one is on the scale of consciousness or human development:[37]

1. Shame: The bum is dirty, shameful, and disgusting.

2. Guilt: The bum is a lazy welfare cheat and hence should be blamed for his condition.

3. Hopelessness: The bum's plight represents the failure of society.

TABLE 6.1. Stages of human development

Levels	Maslow	Hawkins	Levels of moral development (Kohlberg, Gilligan)	Nature of response (Valliant)	Examples
1	Physiological safety	Shame Guilt Fear Anger Pride	Pre-conventional (me, selfish care) Obedience and punishment (I don't want to go to jail) Self-interest (You scratch my back, I will scratch yours)	Defense	Wall Street's confidence that its risk models work just fine AIG executives' spa trips and paying themselves huge bonuses The Chinese government's initial denial of SARS
2	Belonging Self-esteem	Hopelessness Grief Desire	Conventional (us, care) Good boy/nice girl (What will my family and friends say?) Law and order (Is it legal?)	Cope	LTCM's collapse as the result of a low-probability event they ignored in their models Exxon's reducing of safety and maintenance cost because they believed the likelihood of a major spill in the Bay of Valdez was "only once in 241 years"
3	Self-actualization	Courage Neutrality Willingness Reason Acceptance Peace	Post-conventional (all of us, universal care) Social contract (Let's change the laws) Universal ethical principle (Context independent, timeless principles)	Accept	After the murders at a local McDonald's restaurant in San Ysidro, the company's decision to do what is right for the survivors and the families Johnson & Johnson's holding of the interests of potential and actual Tylenol crisis victims always above the interests of shareholders

4. Grief: The bum is a tragic old man without friends and family.

5. Fear: The bum is a threatening social menace; therefore, the police need to be called.

6. Desire: Why doesn't someone do something about him?

7. Anger: The bum might be violent, or we ought to be furious that such conditions exist in a country as rich as ours.

8. Pride: The bum lacks the self-respect to improve himself.

9. Courage: Perhaps all he needs is another chance.

10. Neutrality: "Live and let live," he's not hurting anyone.

11. Willingness: Maybe we just need to talk with him.

12. Acceptance: Maybe he has an interesting story to tell. If we talked to him, what would we learn from him about why he's there?

13. Reason: He's a symptom of the current economic crisis.

14. Higher levels: The old man is friendly and lovable, perhaps he is there voluntarily of his own free will, perhaps he decided to live differently.

15. Peace: The old man is all of us, but only as a temporary manifestation of the Divine.

Hawkins gives an even more powerful example of prisoners who are incarcerated and having their own crisis.[38] Hawkins puts the matter so well that we quote directly:

Placed in an identical and extremely stressful environment [prison], different inmates react in ways that vary extraordinarily according to "where they are coming from." Prisoners whose consciousness is at the lowest end of the scale sometimes attempt suicide in jail; others become psychotic and delusional with guilt. Some fall into despondency, go mute, and stop eating; still others sit with head in hands, trying to hide incipient tears of grief. A common expression is fear, which is manifested either through paranoid defensiveness or blatant sycophancy. Other prisoners react with a great deal of violent and assaultive rage. Pride is everywhere with macho bragging and dominance.

In contrast, some inmates find the courage to face the truth of why they're incarcerated, and begin to look at their lives honestly . . . and there are always those who just "roll with the punches" and try to get some reading done. At the level of Acceptance, we see prisoners who seek out help and join support groups. It isn't unusual for an inmate to take a new interest in learning, perhaps by studying in the prison library, or even becoming a jailhouse lawyer. . . . A few prisoners go through a transformation of consciousness and become loving and generous care-givers to their fellow inmates. And it's not unheard of for a prisoner aligned with higher [states of consciousness] to grow deeply [spiritually], or even to pursue enlightenment. Some even become saintly [one thinks of Nelson Mandela].

Going to prison is a personal crisis for the persons committing the crime and the victims. How one deals with such a crisis is an indicator of one's level of development.

There are at least three broad levels of development. At the low-est levels, crises and messes are either one's fault or something to be blamed on someone else. Morality is defined very narrowly: what is morally right is that which maximizes pleasure and minimizes pain for one's self ("It's not my fault," "I don't want to go to jail," and so on). This is the most immature or primitive level of defense mecha-nisms; in addition to denial, projection, and splitting, this level may also include defenses such as idealization ("Our risk models work just fine") and acting out ("exorbitant spa trips for AIG executives and paying themselves huge bonuses").[39]

At higher levels, defense mechanisms become coping mechanisms. For example, at lower to intermediate levels, defenses include ra-tionalization ("Our size will protect us from crises"), displacement ("Employees who bring bad news deserve to be punished"), and in-tellectualization ("The probability of a mega-crisis happening and affecting us is extremely small, and getting prepared for a non-event is a waste of time and resources").[40]

At even higher levels, defense and coping mechanisms are replaced by acceptance mechanisms. Responses at these levels may
include anticipation ("Crisis management is as important as strategic
management") and altruism ("The interests of potential and actual
crisis victims always dominate the interests of our shareholders").[41]

At the highest levels, mega-messes are no longer experienced as
overwhelming. While one is certainly obligated to do everything in
one's power to prevent mega-crises and to manage mega-messes,
crises and messes are accepted as fundamental parts of the fabric
of the universe. From this perspective, mega-messes are neither
inherently good nor inherently bad. They not only represent a
powerful challenge, they are essential to our growth. We develop
by doing everything in our power to prevent future mega-messes
and mega-crises.

There are of course many other frameworks that one could use
as well.[42] The essential point is that key terms (crises, messes, and
so on) vary enormously as we move up the "ladder of human consciousness and development." One thing is also clear. Crisis-prone
organizations are at the bottom of the ladder. And crisis-prepared
organizations are certainly at the level of "courage," for it takes
enormous fortitude to prepare for those things one has not yet experienced or those one may not experience at all.

If implemented correctly and consistently, all of the seven strategies will help an individual or an organization move up various
developmental lines. Nonetheless, how one moves up the ladder
of human consciousness is an important topic that is beyond the
scope of this book. The interested reader is referred to the sources
in the endnotes.[43]

In the next chapter, we especially want to pursue the ideas in
this section further. They provide a unique basis for evaluating some
of the components of an integrated program of crisis management.

CONCLUDING REMARKS

The results of this chapter lend strong support to one of the prime
contentions that was made in Chapter 1. As they currently exist,

economics and finance are founded upon the flimsiest and the most meager base of human emotions. Furthermore, some of the few emotions that are recognized are at the lowest levels of human consciousness and development. Given that emotions are one of the most important parts of messes and crises, we conclude that the paltry base of human emotions upon which economics and finance have "chosen" to build their theories is an important contributor to the current great financial crisis.

Theories are no better than the base upon which they are built. If the base is seriously flawed, then all the mathematical sophistication in the world will not make up for it.

7   BEYOND FEAR-BASED

CRISIS MANAGEMENT

On Sunday, March 15th, [Treasury Secretary Timothy] Geithner was summoned to the White House for a meeting with the President . . . about whether Obama should adopt Geithner's plan [to entice the private sector to take bad loans off the balance sheet of struggling banks]—or scrap it and come up with something else. . . . Geithner had a line that he often used that summed up how he and his colleagues at Treasury would prevail: "Plan beats no plan." The meeting lasted seven hours. Obama's advisors were so divided that he left them in the Roosevelt Room after the first two hours, saying, "You guys work this out, and when I come back I want you to tell me what your *agreed-upon approach* is" [emphasis added].

—RYAN LIZZA, "Inside the Crisis," *New Yorker*, October 12, 2009

In both the mosaic and in early Christian theology, space was discontinuous. Regions were connected, however, on a grander spiritual level. This higher order reunited the separate individuals of Christendom and the fragmented medieval spaces into a seamless continuum. Each piece of the mosaic is a small part; the sum of the parts makes up a whole that is greater than the totality of the individual pieces.

—LEONARD SHLAIN, *Art and Physics*

THE DOMINANT, PREVAILING FORMS of crisis management are based primarily on fear, denial, and anxiety—in other words, the lower levels of human consciousness. As a consequence, they focus on the small, limited, and seemingly more manageable aspects of crises or messes while ignoring the systemic nature and interconnectedness of these crises.

To manage messes and crises effectively, the first step is to acknowledge and treat the fears and anxieties they trigger. In the previous chapter, we discussed several strategies for overcoming negative emotions and feelings. Although learning to cope with the emotional component of messes and crises is a necessary first step away from fear-based crisis management, by itself it is not sufficient.

To move beyond fear-based crisis management necessitates that we change fundamentally the ways in which we inquire about problems, and even more basic, that we change not only the methods by which we produce knowledge but what we consider to be "knowledge."

This chapter discusses the concept of inquiry systems. Specifically, it argues that crisis management requires that we think systemically. The inquiry system for accomplishing this is named, appropriately, systems thinking.

TOWARD HIGHER FORMS OF CRISIS MANAGEMENT

To move beyond fear-based crisis management, we need to examine what crisis management would look like if it rested on principles at the higher ends of the spectrum of human consciousness.

To accomplish this, we want to look at five fundamentally different inquiry systems or ways of producing knowledge and making decisions. Each system is grounded in a distinct philosophy of knowledge and action. Moreover, the systems can be located at different stages of human consciousness.

However, before we can do this, we need to look at the various components or programs of crisis management. More specifically, we want to examine the following:

1. Crisis communications (CC)

2. Emergency preparedness (EP)

3. Business recovery (BR)

4. High reliability organizations (HROs)

These four have been chosen not only because they are easily mistaken to be the "essence or whole" of crisis management but because they create the illusion that an organization is crisis prepared if one enacts one or more of them. As a result, practitioners often tend to reduce the whole of crisis management to one or more of these four programs.

A more comprehensive and systemic model of the "whole" of crisis management is presented in Figure 7.1.[1]

Figure 7.1 shows how the various components and programs of crisis management fit in relationship to one another. Each of the programs in Figure 7.1 is necessary, but by itself is not sufficient for an effective program or system of crisis management.[2] Of course, these are not the only components or programs of crisis manage-

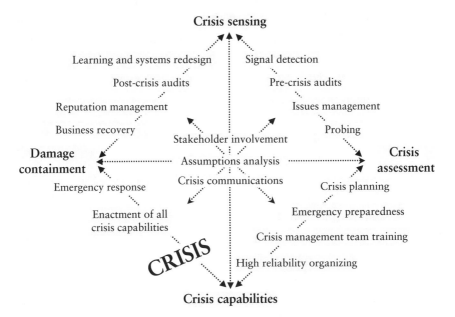

FIGURE 7.1. A systems model of crisis management

ment, but they are the major ones that have been developed and practiced thus far.

More often than not, the various programs are adopted independently of one another. Unfortunately, the forms of crisis management that are motivated by the urge to alleviate fears and worries either ignore altogether the whole represented in Figure 7.1 or focus on those programs that constitute a small subset of Figure 7.1. What follows is a brief critique of the most frequently adopted programs of crisis management.

Crisis Communications

Mostly the large public relations (PR) firms sell crisis communications (CC). Virtually every large PR firm has a substantial crisis management division or department. But, to put it mildly, there is a huge difference between what the PR firms mean by crisis management and what we mean by it.

Typically, PR firms are called in *after* a major crisis has occurred. The primary emphasis is on what and how to communicate to important stakeholders such as the media, customers, suppliers, and so on. The primary emphasis is also on damage containment, that is, how to contain the inevitable damage as the result of a major crisis, especially if the organization is in any way responsible for the crisis and it has resulted in major deaths, serious injuries, severe financial loss, or negative publicity. As such, CC is mainly reactive, in other words, after the fact.

To be fair, the major PR firms often do try hard to sell proactive crisis management in the form of media training to the top executives of large organizations so that both the executives and their organizations will be prepared *before* a significant crisis strikes. The major PR firms know that the heat of a crisis is the worst time to train executives in effective CC.

The main defect of CC is the presumption that one can train high-level executives and managers, let alone their "spokespersons," to "communicate effectively" independently of a deep understanding of the total systems that constitute large multinational organizations and of the full range of emotions that crises trigger. To pretend that crisis management can be reduced to "effective communications," or any other component for that matter, is a gross misunderstanding as to what it is.

Effective crisis management is not a set of generic crisis plans, abstract procedures, and processes that sit on shelves. Instead, like any other activity that an organization regards as key to its very survival and continued success, it is *a program of actual capabilities and processes* that have been practiced over and over again. If these capabilities and processes are not developed, practiced, and improved on constantly prior to the occurrence of major crises, then they are virtually impossible to develop and to enact during the heat of a major crisis, thus adding further to the crisis. (As we write, British Petroleum "has experienced" [that is, "is responsible for"] one of the largest oil spills in history. It is more than evident that the majority of BP's responses are reactive, showing once again that one cannot invent damage containment on the fly.) To use an analogy, although it is far from perfect, we don't send soldiers into battle without first giving them basic training. To lower the physical and mental consequences and hazards of war, we put soldiers through constant simulations and training exercises that are as realistic as possible. "One-shot training programs" (pun intended) fail miserably. For this reason, merely to give executives advance training in CC—that is, in a single aspect of crisis management— may do more harm than good. It feeds the illusion (delusion?) that they are trained in crisis management when they are not. But given the enormous denial that has to be overcome before one can truly engage in effective crisis management, little wonder why CC has been gobbled up by corporate America.

The most serious criticism of CC is that for all its pretensions to the contrary, it does not truly base communications on the upper reaches of the spectrum of human development. There is all the difference in the world between feigning reverence for human life and the environment and actually embodying it. Serious and deep reverence for human life and the environment is "lived," not merely "communicated." It is "spoken" every day in what an organization actually does over the long run.

Nonetheless, we do not doubt for one minute that CC is a *vital part* of every serious program of crisis management.[3] The key phrase is "vital part." CC is not the whole or necessarily even the most important part.

Emergency Preparedness and Business Recovery

Emergency preparedness (EP) and business recovery (BR) are quite different in practice, but because they share the same goals and philosophy, they share similar strengths and weaknesses as well. Thus we shall discuss EP and BR together. Many companies and organizations "buy into" EP and BR. Indeed, second only to CC, EP and BR are among the most popular programs in corporate America. If these are the only programs that companies buy into and they are not part of a comprehensive crisis management strategy, the reasons are best understood in terms of denial.

If mega-crises and mega-messes generally provoke mega-anxiety, then anything that will reduce this anxiety is sorely welcomed and embraced. EP and BR lower anxiety by first reducing the types of crises one needs to think about and hence to prepare for, mainly to physical crises such as fires, explosions, floods, earthquakes, and so on. Second, EP and BR also lower anxiety by saying that one primarily needs only to recover physical places of manufacturing, working, and so on. Thus the psychological aspects of recovery that can actually be much higher in costs and longer term tend to be ignored and overlooked—in other words, denied altogether.

Once again, we do not deny that EP and BR are important, and therefore need to be *vital parts* of any program in crisis management.[4] But they are just parts. In addition, by focusing mainly on the physical aspects of crises, EP and BR are also not high up on the spectrum of consciousness. They do not take into account and therefore treat higher-order needs. They fail to focus on psychological preparedness and the recovery of individuals and organizations.

High Reliability Organizations

The concept of high reliability organizations (HROs) was first formulated in response to organizations whose technologies were so critical that if they failed then huge and terrible consequences would result.[5] Such organizations include nuclear power plants, chemical refineries, hospitals, aircraft carriers, and so on. Since then, the concept of HROs has been extended to offshore oil rigs, electric power plants, metropolitan subway systems, and the like.

The strength of HROs as a concept is that it forces one to study intensively the specific elements that allow complex systems to be operated safely and reliably. In this regard, as we show in the next chapter, there is much that the financial system can learn from the literature on HROs.

Although there is much that organizations in all industries can learn from HROs, the main limitation of the literature on HROs is that thus far it has not focused on types of crises beyond physical ones. It has also failed to look beyond structural variables such as system complexity and interdependence among systems components. For instance, moral and ethical lapses that can lead or at least contribute to physical disasters (think of the *Challenger* and *Columbia* disasters among others) are virtually never discussed in the literature on HROs. For this reason, the concept of HROs is still not high up on the ladder of human development as well. In other words, all of the lessons learned from the HROs are useful, but the concept of HROs must not be mistaken for the whole of crisis management.

As noted, the main critique of these programs is simply that although each is a necessary part of a systemic model of crisis management, they are not the whole. Therefore the question still remains unanswered: What *is* the whole of crisis management? How can we know that Figure 7.1 is a good enough representation of the whole of crisis management? We turn next to these questions.

INQUIRY SYSTEMS

Step by step, the discussion has led us to systems, knowledge, and systems separability, in other words, to what is or is not "part" of a system. Even more basic, what should or should not be regarded as "natural parts" of a system? The same questions may be asked by replacing the word *system* with the word *mess*: What is or is not "part" of a mess? What should or should not be regarded as "natural parts" of a mess?

The concept of inquiry systems is one of the most powerful ways that humans have invented for approaching the foregoing topics. In essence, inquiry systems are fundamentally different ways of obtaining knowledge about the world.

Inquiry systems not only differ basically over what they regard worthy of the honorific term *knowledge*, they differ over what they regard as "valid ways of thinking about anything, including thinking itself." They also differ over what they regard as the "valid boundaries of a 'system.'" That is, they differ fundamentally with respect to "systems separability."

Although there are certainly many more, we want to restrict the discussion to five very different inquiry systems or ways of producing knowledge and thereby of "thinking about thinking."[6] Each inquiry system represents historically a different philosophical method and school for obtaining knowledge. More important, each system is "best suited" for a different aspect of crisis management. Stronger still, each system represents a different stage of human consciousness, development, or both.

A PROSAIC EXAMPLE

To ground the discussion and to make it as concrete and accessible as possible, we are going to talk about inquiry systems in terms of a fictitious company, Healthy Bars Inc. Healthy Bars Inc. is in fact an example that we have used successfully with many different groups to explain the nature and the relevancy of philosophy to their careers and lives.

As its name indicates, Healthy Bars Inc. makes healthy food energy bars. Its goal is not only to be the number one company in its industry in terms of market share but also to be the company that consumers think of first when they think of an environmentally responsible and ethical company.

To increase awareness of its products in order to boost sales, Healthy Bars Inc. decided to hold a worldwide contest. It invited consumers to send in recipes for "how to make the perfect fruit bar."[7] The only restriction was that the recipes had to use one of Healthy Bars Inc.'s products. Other than this, consumers were free to add any ingredients they wished, providing of course that they were safe, environmentally friendly, and legal. The contest winner was to receive not only free health bars for a year but, more important, the honorific title of "master chef."

Although at first glance this example seems trite and far removed from such exalted ideas as systems and truth, let alone human consciousness and crisis management, as we shall see, it is anything but.

The First Way of Deciding: Expert Consensus
Like most organizations, Healthy Bars Inc. appointed a small committee to judge the entries it received. To its chagrin, the committee soon found that it was literally drowning in entries. Thousands of them poured in from all over the world.

The committee was completely stymied. There was no way that a small group could sift through thousands of submissions.

Besides, what was the meaning of "perfect"? They hadn't even considered that a definition of what they were looking for might be important before they started the contest. Rather naively, they thought that it would just emerge from the process. (Recall from Chapter 2 that it is only in exercises and well-structured problems that we start at the beginning of an inquiry with a clear definition of what the problem is. Furthermore, the initial definition does not vary over the course of the inquiry. This is not the case with "real problems.")

One of the members of the committee suggested using a team of their assistants to tabulate all the entries by putting them into a computer. The particular recipe receiving the most votes or the one that had the most in common with all the individual recipes—the "average"—would be declared the winner, in this case, the "perfect fruit bar." The member pointed out that this was a convenient way of bypassing the definition of "perfect." "Perfect" would in effect emerge from the process itself. As the particular member who suggested the idea remarked, "Why get hung up on definitions?"

However, as soon as this was suggested, it raised more concerns and issues than it settled. Most of the committee members felt that it was a complete cop-out. They also worried that it could set off a hailstorm of protests and hence create a crisis for the company. Thus instead of building a favorable image for Healthy Bars, it could cause irreparable damage.

Why was the "average" in any sense the definition of "perfect"? Couldn't it lead to the selection of the most bland and inoffensive entry? Besides, what did it mean to "average" entries from around the world? Were all entries equal? Was everyone who submitted an entry an "expert"? Were all experts equal?

In effect, *the committee couldn't agree among themselves on the method of agreement to use to settle the contest*! Thus this particular method was rejected before it even got started. (In other words, the taken-for-granted and implicit assumption that the problem was well structured was false. In short, it was not a simple exercise.)

Even if they polled "experts" for their opinions, there would still be problems. For instance, how would they define an expert? If an "expert" was defined as a "member 'in good standing' of the community" of "distinguished chefs" worldwide, say all those working in two-star restaurants or better, the committee still felt that this way of choosing the winner would be inadequate, for it would privilege a certain group of experts over all others. In using experts, one is not only dependent on the consensus among them for producing "truth" in the first place—in this case "'truth' is the 'perfect' fruit bar"—one is also assuming that the more agreement there is among the experts, the stronger and therefore the "better" the "truth." In this system, "truth" is that with which a group of experts agrees strongly.

Appropriately enough, this approach is known as the Expert Consensus Way of Knowing or of Producing Knowledge (for short, we will refer to this inquiry system as Expert Agreement). According to this approach, the guarantor of "truth" is both the product and the outcome of the agreement among the judgments, observations, or opinions of different experts.[8] In science, Expert Agreement takes the form of "tight agreement" among the data, facts, or observations produced by independent and well-qualified experts and observers. Take global warming as an example. The body of "reputable scientists worldwide" is now in substantial agreement that human activities are a significant factor responsible for global warming. This "fact" is taken as "strong evidence" that the debate over whether humans are or are not responsible for global warming is essentially over, even if all the mechanisms for it are not understood completely.

Agreement is no less important in science than in any field of human activity. One could in fact argue that agreement is even more important in science, where so much is riding on the outcome of scientific knowledge.

Notice carefully that this method seriously breaks down for mega-messes and mega-crises. By definition, mega-messes and mega-crises are not composed of sets (systems) of problems that are either well structured or independent of one another. This does not mean that one cannot and should never collect data about the components of messes and crises. It merely means that one cannot hope to understand and to treat messes and crises solely or completely by the method of Expert Agreement.

As a result of its obsessive need for certainty and control, Expert Agreement, as a form of inquiry, is automatically at the lower end of the ladder of human development. Indeed, one can in fact contend that it is a form of inquiry that is rooted deeply in a kind of fear, the fear of losing control. Little wonder why that its proponents often proclaim vociferously that anything not living up to its tight standards is automatically to be dismissed as inferior, and therefore not to be taken seriously.

The Second Way of Deciding: "The One True Formula!"

One of the committee members had a B.S. in chemistry from a top university. She argued that chemistry should be used to derive the ingredients and the recipe for the perfect fruit bar. The winner of the contest would be the person or persons whose submission matched the recipe derived by means of this procedure.

In the second system or model of inquiry, the perfect recipe is based on the theoretical principles and laws of some "hard science" such as chemistry and that particular science alone. Thus, in this system, science is *the model* for inquiry, and "truth" is equivalent to a single, clear, well-structured formula.

The reasoning behind this model is that "the perfect fruit bar"— truth itself—should not be based on anything so crass as the mere opinions of a group of experts no matter how distinguished they may be. Truth shouldn't even be based on what a particular set of experts regard as the "facts," because the "facts" of one group and of one age have an uncanny way of becoming the falsehoods of another. After all, it was once an agreed-upon "fact" that the Earth was flat.

Truth should be based on the established principles—the laws— of hard science. In fact, proceeding from firmly established scientific first principles, one should be able to derive a single formula. For instance, in the case of a falling body, the distance D that it covers in a certain amount of time T is given by the familiar formula $D = (1/2)GT^2$, where G equals the acceleration due to gravity. That is, the formula is familiar to those who have taken a basic course in physics. Since the formula for falling bodies can be derived directly from Newton's law of gravitation—one of the first principles of physical science—the formula is akin to a "hard law of nature." (That is, those who understand differential calculus can derive it.) The important point is that this system seeks to produce a single abstract formula that it regards as "the truth."

Appropriately enough, this system is known as the Pure Theory Way of Knowing. For short, we refer to it as the One True Formula.

This system is actually much broader than mathematics or

science alone. Much more basic, and perhaps subtle, is the idea that the One True Formula is a coherent belief system—a framework of basic, presumably rational, first principles. In this broader sense, it does not always appear in the form of a formula. Although he was probably unaware of it, writing in *Time* magazine, Michael Kinsley expressed the notion as follows:

Ideology is a good thing, not a bad one—and partisanship is at its worst when it is not about ideology. That's when it descends into trivia and slime. Ideology doesn't have to mean mindless intransigence or a refusal to accommodate new evidence or changing evidence. *It is just a framework of basic principles. A framework is more than a list: all the pieces should fit together [coherently]* [emphasis added].[9]

Needless to say, the committee didn't buy this way of choosing the winner as well. Why should the winner be decided by a single scientific discipline, let alone something so ridiculous as a single formula? Why was chemistry superior to any other science, or for that matter, any nonscientific discipline or profession such as cooking? If one was restricted to choosing a single discipline, why shouldn't it be psychology? Weren't the attitudes of the contestants just as important as the physical ingredients themselves?

Since the committee couldn't answer their own questions on the basis of their own first principles (pun intended), they rejected the method of first principles in choosing the winner.

Notice once again that this approach doesn't work *entirely* for mega-messes and mega-crises for the very same reasons that were given earlier as to why Expert Agreement also breaks down.

There is another serious flaw of both Expert Agreement and the One True Formula.

Expert Agreement assumes that we can just "open our eyes" and gather data or observations without presupposing any prior theories, presumptions, or values. In other words, data are independent or separable from theory and values. What this ignores is the "fact" that we never gather data or observations randomly but always with some ends in mind. However informal and unconscious our ends may be, they serve nonetheless as "informal guides or theories." Even more, they express our taken-for-granted values.

By the same token, the One True Formula assumes that the building of theories is independent of data in that it is purely an exercise in pure logic or thought alone. This too ignores the "fact" that time and time again it has been shown that historical, personal, and social factors affect what are regarded as "good theories," let alone how such theories are built by all-too-human beings.

The Third Way of Deciding:
Multiple Perspectives, Multiple Formulas

One of the committee members suggested an approach that all of the members agreed with instantly. For the first time, they felt that they were making headway. (Notice that in agreeing so readily, they were buying into the first method, Expert Agreement. In effect, they were using the first way of producing knowledge to select another way of producing it.[10] There is nothing inherently wrong with combining inquiry systems. This is in fact an important way of getting around the weaknesses of any single system. The "truth" no longer depends or rests upon a single system.)

Instead of lumping all of the entries together and averaging them, suppose that one grouped them initially by countries or regions of the world. Or, suppose that one first grouped them by different schools or philosophies of cooking. Then, from each group, one could select a winner by using the first way of knowing, consensus.[11]

Another way to put it is to say that instead of there being a single, best formula for all of the entries, suppose that each group of entries had its own special formula. Using each formula, one would determine the winners of each group, and from these, one would select an overall winner.

The third system is a combination of the first two: Expert Agreement and the One True Formula. In this approach, backed up by whatever data and facts they have to support their judgments, one samples the opinions of different regions or schools of cooking. Presumably, each region or school has its own distinct recipe or formula.

This system allows a decision maker to witness explicitly how the outcome, the perfect fruit bar, varies as one changes the underlying method or formula (recipe) for producing it. It thus allows a decision maker—in this case, the committee members, who may not be experts in, or proponents of, any particular school of cooking—to better understand the reasoning behind each school by seeing how they each approach the "same problem."

This system allows one to see explicitly the differences between various approaches. In other words, it does not leave variety to chance. Unlike the first two ways, it does not believe that there is one best answer to complex problems or questions. To the contrary! According to this approach, the guarantor of "truth" is the *range* of different perspectives that are produced on a problem.

The third way believes that on any problem of importance, one must produce *at least two* different views of the problem (or mess or crisis) if one is even to begin to ascertain whether one is committing a type three error, with "type three error" defined as solving the wrong problem precisely. Unless we have two or more different formulations of a problem, we cannot possibly know whether we are solving the "wrong" or the "right" problem, or working on the "right" components of a mess and its interactions. Without two or more views to compare, the terms *right* and *wrong* have no meaning, unless of course one believes unequivocally in the "truth" of a single system or way of looking at the world.

This system is thus a minimal requirement for ascertaining whether we are committing type three errors. It is also a minimal requirement for working on mega-messes and mega-crises.

One can also begin to understand why the third way of knowing is the basis of critical thinking: in effect, thinking about thinking. It forces one to examine the assumptions and values that underlie any particular formulation of a problem, mess, or crisis by explicitly comparing different formulations by different stakeholders. After one has witnessed the differences between different approaches, one can, if one wishes, pick and choose—blend if need be—among them to form one's own unique recipe.

Appropriately enough, this system is known as the Multiple Perspective or the Multiple Formula Approach to Knowledge. It argues that complex problems are too important to be left to the reasoning of any single approach no matter how appealing that approach is. The more that a particular approach is appealing, the more one needs to resist the temptation to fall under its sway.

This system is also known as Multidisciplinary Inquiry. The end result of this form of inquiry is a conclusion or recommendation that is the product of two or more scientific disciplines or professions. For instance, a purely technical explanation of the explosion of the space shuttle *Challenger*, that it was caused by faulty O-rings, is not sufficient. One must pick at least one more additional perspective to examine the interactions between the technical causes and others such as the culture of NASA (anthropology) or the politics surrounding the launch (political science or sociology).

Finally, there is another aspect of this system that is very important to note. Recall that the first two systems assume that data (expert judgments, facts, observations) and theory are independent of one another. In contrast, the third system assumes that our prior beliefs and values affect what we decide is important to collect or to observe. Every observation we make presumes that we have made a decision about what is worth observing. The upshot is that not only are data, facts, and observations not theory free, they certainly are not value free.

Ethics is thus an important part of every inquiry, whether we acknowledge it or not. In fact, the less we acknowledge it, the more important it is, because instead of examining and debating our ethical assumptions, the more we take them for granted.

In sum, in this system, ethics, theory, and data are highly inseparable.

The Fourth Way of Deciding: Expert Disagreement

Someone on the committee had another idea. Instead of depending upon the *agreement* among experts, suppose they used *disagreement*. The winner of a debate between experts would then be the winner of the contest.

The fourth approach is the direct opposite of the first. Whereas consensus is the guarantor of the perfect fruit bar and the way to produce "truth" in the first approach, intense conflict is the guarantor and the way to obtain "truth" in the fourth model.

In the fourth approach, one picks two schools of cooking that disagree the most. One then arranges a knockdown, no-holds-barred debate between them. The recipe that emerges from (survives) the debate, which may be neither of the original two recipes, is then dubbed the "truth." (The cult TV program *Iron Chef* is an example of this approach.) Appropriately, this model is known as the Dialectical Theory or Model of Knowledge. It is also known as the Conflict Theory of Truth, or Expert *Dis*agreement for short.

To show how the fourth approach applies to business, and in essence to all professions, consider the following: Alfred P. Sloan, chairman of General Motors from 1937 to 1956, is one of the very few executives who not only understood the importance of the fourth way but actually used it when he had an important decision to make. When his top executives agreed too quickly and too readily with his ideas, Sloan is reputed to have said, "I propose we postpone further discussion until our next meeting to give ourselves time to develop disagreement and perhaps gain some understanding of what the decision is all about."[12]

Notice that the Myers-Briggs framework that we introduced in Chapter 1 encourages one to adopt both the third and the fourth ways of knowing. The quadrants are good examples of multiple perspectives. Each perspective provides a fundamentally different definition of a mess or a crisis. For instance, in the context of the health care crisis, each quadrant provides a different piece of the mess: the upper left focused on cost-containment, the upper right on innovation, the lower left on personal concerns, and the lower right on societal values.

The quadrants are also good examples of strong disagreements. The vertical and horizontal dimensions (parts versus whole, individual versus collective, technical versus social, present versus future, short-term versus long-term, and so on) tap into some of the most fundamental axes of disagreements among stakeholders and trade-offs stakeholders must face. For instance, an expert who focuses on finding a fix for one of the technical aspects of a crisis (say, the design of the O-rings of the space shuttles) may disagree strongly with another expert who argues that unless the culture of NASA is changed, similar accidents will happen in the future. The first expert's rationale is, "The shuttles had been operated successfully for many years. If the O-rings weren't faulty, we wouldn't have lost a shuttle. If there is no technical problem, shuttles will keep operating, regardless of the culture. A shuttle's failure is a technical issue." The second expert's rationale is, "First we lost *Challenger*, next we lost *Columbia*. Yes, both accidents were caused by technical problems. It was an O-ring problem for *Challenger*, and it was due to foam for *Columbia*. But because of NASA's culture both problems were ignored and not properly addressed. If NASA's culture does not change, we will lose another shuttle because of another technical problem ignored by the organization. The failures are as much a cultural issue."

Note that none of the quadrants or perspectives of Myers-Briggs provides the "right" definition or solution to the mess or crisis. But as a whole, the Myers-Briggs framework creates higher levels of awareness of a mess or crisis. This is not to say that the Myers-Briggs framework is complete. It merely provides the minimum number of perspectives one needs to take to confront a mess and the most fundamental dimensions about which people tend to disagree strongly.

It is only with the help of the fourth way that we truly understand and appreciate messes and crises. This approach allows us to understand the deep-seated assumptions that stakeholders make about themselves, others, and the messes around them. According to the fourth way, the effective management of messes and crises requires that assumptions be exposed, understood, critiqued, and, if necessary, changed.

It is true that the third way also reveals different assumptions. But these assumptions are not challenged directly and thus they may remain unchanged. The fourth way is about direct confrontation. It deals with assumptions at a deeper, emotional level. If people want to avoid the third way, it may be because of their fear of complexity. But if people want to avoid the fourth way, it is often because of their fear of conflict or confronting their own problems. Only at this level does one understand the essence of Chapter 6: mega-denial. One's fears and anxieties must be dealt with explicitly if one is to move beyond fear-based crisis management.

The Fifth Way of Deciding: Systems Thinking
The committee still weren't satisfied. They still felt that something fundamental was missing, but they didn't know exactly what it was. Experts were fallible. Formulas didn't work. Even debates among experts weren't enough. There seemed to be no precise way of solving this problem. Someone finally exclaimed, "We need help."

With this, another person added, "We're thinking too narrowly. We need to expand our thinking." This led her to say, "Maybe we need to bring in someone who can help us to think more broadly. Isn't this what systems thinking is all about? Why don't we call in a systems expert?"

The last way of knowing is the most comprehensive of all. It is known as the Systems Way of Thinking, or simply Systems Thinking.

In the fifth model, one sweeps in not only the first four models, but also considerations that are typically overlooked by them. In this model, ethical and aesthetic considerations are never ignored, nor considered solely as "just another perspective." They are given center stage. For example, using the "right" (that is, "ethical" or "sustainable") ingredients that are not harmful to the environment is central in this approach. For another, the ambience or the aesthetic design of the kitchen in which a fruit bar is produced is as important as the actual physical recipe itself. In fact, anything that affects the mental state and the well-being of the chef is potentially an essential part of the "recipe"—for example, the lighting and the color of the walls of the kitchen, and so on. Furthermore, the level of consciousness or moral development of the chef becomes an extremely important if not a major concern. Whether the perfect recipe is created by an evil genius or not matters.

The fifth model helped to put some of the entries in a special light (pun intended). A few of the entries described the setting in which they prepared their submissions. They felt that the kitchen in which the fruit bars were prepared was as important as the raw ingredients themselves. For this reason, they included pictures of their kitchens along with their recipes. Other entries included the chef's life history, philosophy, and values.

In the end, however, the committee began to question whether or not its goal of becoming the market share leader in its industry was compatible with the goal of becoming an environmentally responsible and ethical company. The fifth model helped the committee move to a higher level of consciousness in which the trade-off between market share and environmental and ethical responsibilities disappeared. The committee decided that if these two goals conflicted, the goal of higher standards of ethics would trump the goal of greater market share.

The fifth and last way of knowing is based on the work of C. West Churchman and his mentor, E. A. Singer Jr.[13] Singer, who was one of William James's best students, emphasized that there are no "basic disciplines or sciences." For Singer and Churchman, no science, no profession or field of knowledge, was more basic than or superior to any other. This idea is so important that it is one of the fundamental cornerstones of systems thinking.

In systems thinking, the physical sciences, certainly knowledge about the physical world, are inseparable from the social sciences and knowledge about the social world. Churchman's philosophy, and that of his life-long friend and colleague Russ Ackoff,[14] is based on Singer's. In their philosophy, the physical and the social sciences are not only inseparable, they presuppose one another. Neither is possible without the other. Once again, whether we admit it or not, physical science is done by all-too-human beings that not only have a "psychology" but operate within a "social context." The psychology and the sociology of the investigator or the "expert" affect not only the production of physical knowledge but its very existence.[15]

The idea that there are no "basic disciplines" is scary for those who believe that there is a distinct hierarchy of the sciences or disciplines. Logic, math, physics, and so on are at the top, and social sciences such as history and anthropology are at the bottom. In the context of the *Challenger* disaster, this is akin to claiming that the most important cause (the "objective" cause) of the explosion was the faulty O-rings. Furthermore, how the O-rings caused the accident has little to do with the culture of NASA, the ethical and moral values of the organizations involved, the cognitive biases and psychology of the engineers and managers, the politics of space shuttle missions, and so on.

THE SUMMARY THUS FAR: OBJECTIVITY

Our discussion of different inquiry systems helps to make clear why the admonition to be "objective" is in most cases laughable if not meaningless. Which *kind* of objectivity is the proper response?

According to Expert Agreement, something is objective if and only if it is based on "hard data, facts, or observations," the "tight agreement" among different observers as to the data, and so on.

According to the One True Formula, something is objective if and only if it is based on logical reasoning from self-evident first principles or premises. The trouble is that as the American humorist Ambrose Bierce observed, "self-evident means evident to one's self and to no one else."

According to Multiple Perspectives, something is objective if and only if it is the product and the result of multiple points of view.

According to Expert Disagreement, something is objective if and only if it is the product and the result (it survives) of the most intense debate between the most disparate points of view.

And finally, in Systems Thinking, something is objective if and only if it is the product and the result of the most intense effort of sweeping in different knowledge from the arts, humanities, professions, philosophy, sciences, and so on. In other words, in Systems Thinking, the notion of inseparability is not only the most developed, but the most far ranging. It thus strives to incorporate the highest rungs of the ladder of human development. In Systems Thinking, it makes no sense to be "objective" without cultivating higher orders of consciousness.

Table 7.1 shows how each inquiry system goes beyond but includes all of the previous inquiry systems.

The most radical conclusion is that it is not possible to manage either mega-messes or mega-crises without cultivating higher stages of consciousness. A corollary is that if one tries to manage mega-messes and mega-crises without cultivating higher stages of consciousness, then one creates more messes and crises.

TABLE 7.1. Inquiry systems and the stages of consciousness or awareness

Inquiry system	Stage of consciousness or awareness
Expert agreement	The guarantor of truth is consensus among experts.
One true formula	Experts are fallible.
	The guarantor of truth is a single, clear, well-structured formula.
Multiple perspectives	Experts are fallible.
	Single, clear, well-structured formulas don't work in all contexts.
	The guarantor of truth is a range of multiple formulas and experts.
Expert disagreement	Experts are fallible.
	Single, clear, well-structured formulas don't work in all contexts.
	Multiple formulas and experts are sometimes inadequate.
	The guarantor of truth is strong disagreement and debates between experts and formulas.
Systems thinking	Experts are fallible.
	Single, clear, well-structured formulas don't work in all contexts.
	Multiple formulas and experts are sometimes inadequate.
	Strong disagreements and debates among experts are sometimes inadequate.
	The guarantor of truth is inseparable from the guarantors of goodness, justice, fairness, and beauty.

THE PROBLEM WITH TRADITIONAL EDUCATION

Traditional education primarily stresses the first two ways of knowing or systems of inquiry: Expert Agreement and the One True Formula. Traditional education pounds into our minds "well-accepted facts" based on the first way of knowing, Expert Agreement, and it stresses knowledge of "well-accepted theories"—the One Best Formula—in solving problems. Anything that cannot be reduced to hard data, facts, or observations—the first way—or represented in terms of accepted theories—the second way—is false, dangerous, and misleading.

The first and second ways are historically the foundations of education and of knowledge for a traditional "round world." But they are seriously deficient and inadequate for a "flat world," that is, a world that is global and increasingly interconnected along every conceivable dimension—in short, a world that is composed of messes from top to bottom. For one, they are too restrictive. They assume that the problems we need to solve are already well known and well defined. But as we have stressed throughout, the "problem" with most problems is "to define what the problem(s) is (are) in the first place." For this reason, the type three error is part and parcel of every problem, and mess, that by definition is "important."

The first two ways are not well suited for complex problems such as the great financial crisis. Indeed, they were parts of problems leading to the mess. Surely, the definition, let alone the resolution, of the crisis is as difficult and as messy as the Iraq War. This is precisely where the third (Multiple Perspectives), the fourth (Expert Disagreement), and the fifth (Systems Thinking) ways are required.

The third way, Multiple Perspectives or Formulas, says that we explicitly need to see multiple definitions of a problem so that we can attempt to avoid type three errors. The fourth way, Expert Disagreement, says that we need to acknowledge and confront our deepest assumptions and beliefs in order to do so.

Notice that comparing two or more different formulations of a problem is not an iron-clad guarantee that we will solve the right problems precisely. At best, it is a minimal guarantor. But we can

say that without examining explicitly two or more different formulations, the probability of committing type three errors goes up
considerably. The third, fourth, and fifth ways require us to exercise judgment, and an even more precious commodity, wisdom. We
have to decide, in our best judgment, which problems can be solved,
resolved, dissolved, or absolved.

CONCLUDING REMARKS

The moral of the story is *not* that we should never use the first two
ways of knowing, but that we should use them only after we have
assured ourselves that, by using the third, fourth, and fifth ways, we
are working on the "right problem" to begin with. The third, fourth,
and fifth ways are best suited for problem formulation; in contrast,
the first two ways are best suited for problem solving.

A complex, globally interconnected world requires that we manage problems—messes—not solve them exactly as we attempted to
do in a simpler, fragmented world. A complex, globally interconnected world also requires that we acknowledge that the predomi-
nant philosophical bases of a simpler, fragmented world—the first
two ways of knowing—do not apply in their entirety. They apply
only in the sense that we still collect data when we can and we still
apply accepted scientific thinking, but we accept their limitations.

In the end, one of the most essential aspects of systems thinking is the realization that we only get out of inquiry what we put
into it initially. And what we fundamentally put into every inquiry
is "ourselves" through our collective psychology.

In far too many cases, we are obsessed with what John Dewey
referred to as "the quest for certainty."[16] The first two ways differ
only in where they locate the certainty we so desperately seek. The
first way, Expert Agreement, attempts to find certainty in hard
data and expert consensus, supposedly the "facts" on which everyone can agree. The second way, the One Best Formula, attempts to
find it in the "indisputable scientific laws of nature, pure thought,
or abstract logic." For Dewey, both were neurotic attempts on the
part of humankind to manage the anxiety brought about by a dan-

gerous and uncertain world into which all of us are born. Notice carefully that Dewey did not say that "basic facts" or "elemental truths" were neurotic in themselves. What was neurotic was our obsessive need for certainty.

The danger is not that we will agree, but that we will agree too readily by being pressured to go along with the crowd.

The words of the noted political columnist E. J. Dionne Jr. provide a fitting conclusion:

Honest to goodness, I truly prefer consensus, civility, and problem-solving. But if there is one thing worse than the absence of bipartisanship, it is a phony and ultimately unstable [first way] consensus that sells out everybody's [second way] principles. For better or worse, we have a lot of fighting and arguing [the fourth way] to do before we can enter the gates of a truly bipartisanship paradise.[17]

PART III APPLICATIONS

8   THE ART AND SCIENCE OF MESSY INQUIRY

T HROUGHOUT THIS BOOK, we have argued that every aspect of mega-messes and mega-crises must be viewed from multiple perspectives. A methodology for accomplishing this is what we mean by "messy inquiry." This chapter outlines the nature of messy inquiry by using it to make sense of the great financial crisis.

While messy inquiry is necessary to diagnose the root causes of mega-messes, we make no claim whatsoever that it is sufficient. We also make no claim that it will necessarily prevent the next mega-crisis. Nonetheless, messy inquiry is indispensable in helping us to understand the general nature (that is, patterns) of mega-messes and mega-crises. It not only helps to provide a partial solution to messes as a whole, it also helps us to avoid solving the wrong problems precisely.

A MESSY INQUIRY SYSTEM

In previous chapters, we argued that any crisis is potentially an economic, an environmental, an international, a legal, a public health, a political, a psychological, and even a religious crisis, to mention only a few. We also argued that every known field of inquiry, discipline,

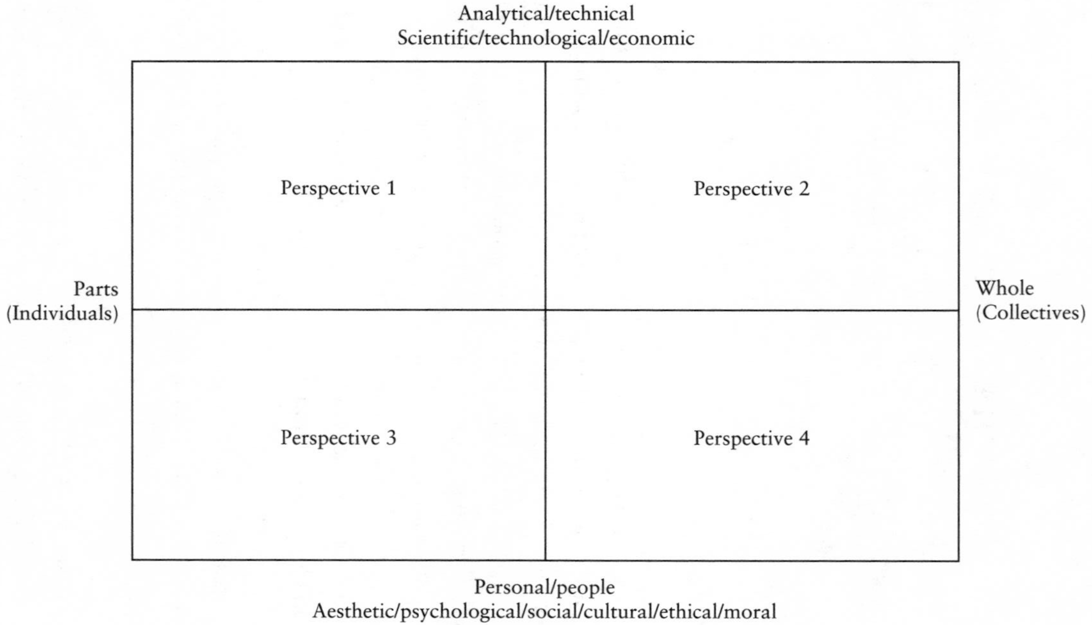

Analytical/technical
Scientific/technological/economic

	Whole (Collectives)
Perspective 1	Perspective 2
Perspective 3	Perspective 4
Parts (Individuals)	

Personal/people
Aesthetic/psychological/social/cultural/ethical/moral

FIGURE 8.1.   A messy inquiry

and profession is needed to confront crises and messes. We have also stressed the need for intense cooperation and deep integration across different fields.

We want to use the Myers-Briggs framework once again to outline a set of critical elements that must be included in what we call a messy inquiry system, or MIS for short. (Our use of the term *MIS* is not meant to coincide with the more common usage, management information system. Or, alternatively, a messy inquiry system is a very different kind of management information system.)

First of all, an MIS must respect different perspectives (disciplines, professions, cultures, and so on). Second, an MIS must not privilege any particular perspective over all others: that is, no perspective has the final say. As a result, an MIS must accept that conflict among different perspectives is a normal and an essential part of inquiry. Third, an MIS must aim to integrate insights from different perspectives into a plausible explanation or narrative about mega-messes and mega-crises. In sum, an MIS must originate from a more inclusive level of awareness and be grounded in the fifth way of knowing, Systems Thinking.

FOUR VERY DIFFERENT PERSPECTIVES

The Myers-Briggs framework that we presented in Chapter 1 is helpful in identifying at least four different perspectives on any issue. Since this chapter uses the framework in a deeper way, we need to explain it differently.

The horizontal axis in Figure 8.1 acknowledges the tension between parts and wholes, or individuals and collectives. The horizontal axis thus helps to identify the "scope" of any problem. Every whole is a part of a larger whole, and every part comprises smaller parts. As there is no "natural end" to larger and larger wholes, there is no natural end to "atoms" or "parts" as well. One can always reduce any problem down into finer and finer parts or atoms.

The definition of an "individual" is not possible without reference to some sort of collective (group, community, society) within which individuals exist (literally "are") and without which they couldn't exist ("be") in the first place. Similarly, the definition of a "collective" presupposes the existence of individuals who constitute the whole. The horizontal axis both highlights the interconnectedness of different aspects of reality and places them on an equal footing: parts and wholes, individuals and collectives. In other words, the horizontal axis reminds us of a very simple yet often ignored point that ideas, things, individuals, organizations, and so on cannot be studied without simultaneously acknowledging their "partness" and "wholeness."

The vertical axis in Figure 8.1 identifies two main "processes" that one can use to deal with any problem. The first process at the top of the vertical axis or dimension focuses on the impersonal, observable, measurable, analytic, technical aspects of problems. The second one focuses on the personal, emotional, cultural, value-laden, and human aspects of problems. Whereas the first process forces an inquirer to view problems from the vantage point of an outsider, the second requires one to view problems from the vantage point of an insider. These two processes capture different aspects of a mess, the totality of which cannot be captured fully using one and only one of these two processes. For example, whereas the upper quadrants acknowledge the scientific, technological, and economic spheres of our lives, the lower quadrants emphasize the moral, ethical, aesthetic, and social spheres.

Combining the vertical and the horizontal axes provides four perspectives, each of which reveals different aspects of mega-messes:

- Perspective 1: an impersonal, technical, scientific approach to the study of parts

- Perspective 2: an impersonal, technical, scientific approach to the study of wholes

- Perspective 3: a personal, social, cultural approach to the study of individuals

- Perspective 4: a personal, social, cultural approach to the study of groups

Each perspective has its own beliefs and assumptions regarding the nature of reality (what is real?) as well as the nature of our knowledge of reality (what do we know and how do we know what we know?).

Although most disciplines and professions have at least one "favorite" perspective, every discipline and profession in one way or another needs all four perspectives if it is to achieve an integrated view(s) of reality. For example, physics, mathematics, and economics (which tend to favor the upper quadrants) are done by people. It is not only naïve but plain false to believe that any discipline is uninfluenced by the lower quadrants (politics, psychological biases, moral values, and so on).[1]

The upper quadrants focus on what is observable and measurable. For example, microeconomics, which studies the behavior and decisions of the smallest parts of an economic system such as households and individual firms, is mostly grounded in perspective 1. At first glance, mainstream macroeconomics typically falls under perspective 2 because it studies the behavior of the economy (or the global economy) as a whole. Nonetheless, because it largely ignores the embeddedness of economics in social structures and cultural practices (that is, lower quadrants),[2] it falls under perspective 1. Laboratory experiments, which are designed to isolate and focus on the relationships among a few controlled and manipulated variables, are also among the favorite methods of the proponents of perspective 1.

The quintessential approach of perspective 2 is systems theory or, more broadly, Systems Thinking, as we outlined in Chapter 7. Systems theory is one of the few approaches that recognizes and appreciates the legitimacy of multiple perspectives. Systems theory basically is a holistic and interdisciplinary framework to study any system such as organisms, organizations, or societies. (Note that organisms and organizations are not the same even though they are often confused with each other. An organization is composed of individuals that can exhibit purpose, in other words, choose different means under different conditions to accomplish an intended goal. Organisms, however, are composed of parts that serve a function and cannot exist outside of the whole system.) It emphasizes the importance of the whole and argues that parts and the interactions among them must and can only be understood in the context of the whole. Another example of perspective 2 is social network analysis,[3] which focuses on the structure of the various "ties" within any network. The unit of analysis is not the parts themselves but the interactions among them and the structure of the interactions.

The lower quadrants focus on the intensely personal experiences and interpretations of individuals within small groups and larger communities. The lower left, or perspective 3, focuses on the experiences and interpretations of the individual. Developmental psychology, which studies how human beings change over time; cognitive psychology, which studies the mind and consciousness; and psychoanalysis, which studies the unconscious, are some of the different approaches to the study of individuals.[4]

Cultural anthropology with its emphasis on ethnographic methodology is one of the best examples of perspective 4. Ethnography assumes that one cannot understand or communicate with individuals without understanding the larger whole or collective of which the individual is a member. This requires that researchers become participant observers (that is, parts of the whole they are studying). Researchers immerse themselves in the context or whole to reveal the meaning and interpretation of everyday experiences.[5]

Obviously, mastering all of the methodologies identified above is a tall order. It is unrealistic for one person or even a single group of people to be competent in ethnography, microeconomics, macroeconomics, experimental method, network analysis, systems theory, developmental psychology, psychoanalysis, and other perspectives we have not mentioned. The direct implication is that a team or community of researchers is necessary to understand and to cope with any mess. All of the perspectives provide an important part of the total picture, and they should be at least acknowledged and considered before jumping to conclusions about any important issue, let alone crises and messes. It is certainly understandable that no one can master all disciplines, but it is not acceptable to deny the validity of all other disciplines.

For example, understanding the mathematical and statistical aspects (upper left) of how financial derivatives work is essential in confronting the current financial mega-mess and mega-crisis. But by itself, this isn't fruitful if one doesn't try to understand the culture of Wall Street (lower right); American consumerism, or equating the pursuit of happiness with consumption (lower left and lower right); the macroeconomic and political swings between capitalism and socialism during the process of globalization (upper right and lower right); the American dream and its connections to homeownership (lower right and lower left); the politics and ideology of homeownership in America (upper right); the cognitive biases of individuals when making economic decisions (lower left); and so on. A properly conducted messy inquiry forces researchers to jump from one quadrant, discipline, or profession to another in order to have a more complete picture of the mess or the crisis at hand.

The point is not that one needs to know everything before one can act, but, to the best of one's ability, one needs to appreciate and to tolerate conflict and complexity in order to avoid solving the wrong problems precisely. (The sophomoric criticism of systems thinking that "one needs to know everything before one can know anything and therefore act" is best viewed for what it is, a defense mechanism to avoid recognizing, studying, and coping with messes.) There are very few guidelines as to which disciplines, professions, approaches, or methodologies to choose for a particular inquiry. The choice may always be more akin to an art than to a science. Nonetheless, one should always strive to pick at least one discipline, profession, and approach from each perspective. In other words, any mess or crisis (or any concept) should be viewed from at least four different perspectives. And the different and often conflicting insights of these four perspectives must be synthesized and integrated.

In the following sections, we use the framework of messy inquiry to analyze the great financial crisis, and by doing so, we will try to achieve a better, if only a partial, understanding and explanation of it.

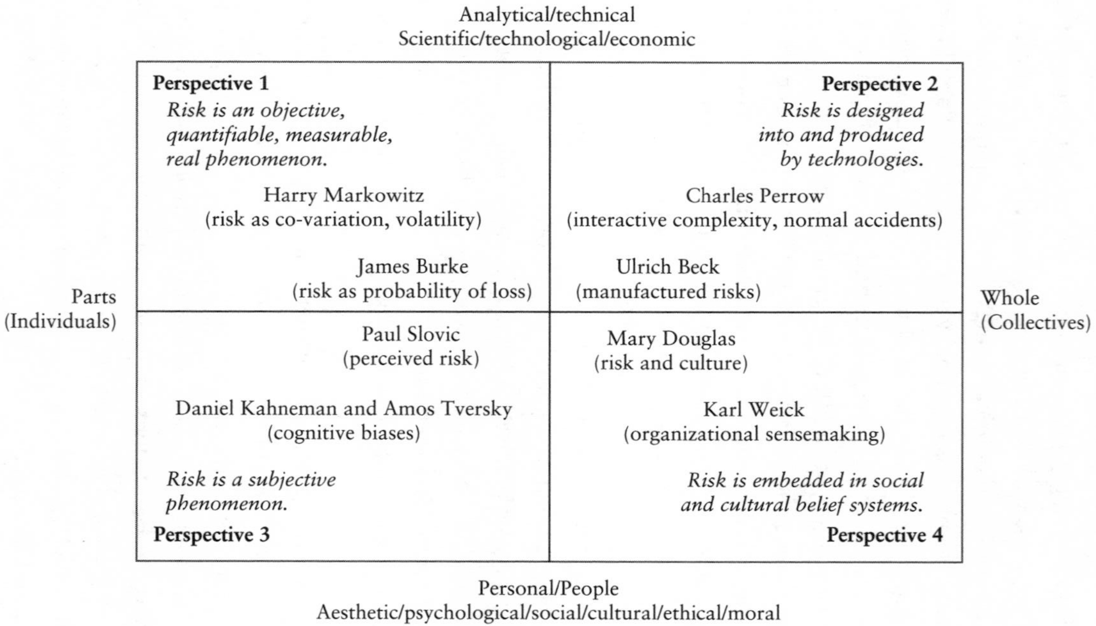

Analytical/technical
Scientific/technological/economic

Whole
(Collectives)

Perspective 1
Risk is an objective,
quantifiable, measurable,
real phenomenon.

Harry Markowitz
(risk as co-variation, volatility)

James Burke
(risk as probability of loss)

Perspective 2
Risk is designed
into and produced
by technologies.

Charles Perrow
(interactive complexity, normal accidents)

Ulrich Beck
(manufactured risks)

Mary Douglas
(risk and culture)

Karl Weick
(organizational sensemaking)

Risk is embedded in social
and cultural belief systems.
Perspective 4

Paul Slovic
(perceived risk)

Daniel Kahneman and Amos Tversky
(cognitive biases)

Risk is a subjective
phenomenon.
Perspective 3

Parts
(Individuals)

Personal/People
Aesthetic/psychological/social/cultural/ethical/moral

FIGURE 8.2.   A messy inquiry into risk

THE FINANCIAL MEGA-MESS

No one variable or perspective can explain the current financial mess. Thus several factors are necessary in order to weave together a satisfactory explanation of certain aspects of the financial mega-mess. As a result, we will not explain a few factors in depth and linearly. On the contrary, we will try to show the relevance of multiple factors. We will use the concept of "risk" to organize, integrate, and weave together the various explanations.

A Messy Inquiry into "Risk"

To understand the great financial crisis, we need to understand "risk as a messy concept," the misunderstanding of which has contributed greatly to the current crisis. Figure 8.2 presents four fundamental perspectives on risk. Each quadrant contains a very different definition of risk.[6]

The upper left quadrant (perspective 1) focuses on the so-called, presumed objective, identifiable, and "real" aspects of risk.[7] In this view or perspective, risk can be measured and quantified in at least two different ways: by calculating the volatility or variance of a measurable variable (such as the value of a portfolio) around its mean value or the correlations among multiple measurable variables (such as asset prices in a portfolio),[8] and by multiplying the probability of an event by the magnitude of its consequences, which are also real, measurable, and quantifiable.[9]

The upper right quadrant (perspective 2) views risk as a direct consequence of the interactions between highly complex and tightly coupled technologies, markets, organizations, and even societies.[10] That is, risk is produced, and in this sense "manufactured," by humans and the things they create and maintain. In the process of trying to eliminate risk, it then becomes a key design constraint. As we aim to create technologies, markets, and organizations that will not put us at risk, we often create more and unforeseen risks.[11]

The lower quadrants have a markedly different approach to the definition of risk. The lower left quadrant (perspective 3) views risk as a "personal" phenomenon. As such, it focuses on human emotions, cognitive limits, cognitive biases, and the notion of "perceived" risk.[12] In short, risk *is* "perceived risk."

The lower right quadrant (perspective 4) focuses on the embeddedness of risk in social and cultural belief systems. In this quadrant, risk is interpretative.[13] It is constructed as we try to make sense of the safety, reliability, and so on of our technologies and organizations.[14]

Risky Assumptions

It is not an exaggeration in the least to say that the vast majority of, if not virtually all, departments of economics and finance (EFDs) are obsessed with various forms of *reductionism*, that is, reducing wholes into parts. Thus, in many EFDs, perspective 1, with its emphasis on math, logic, measurement, quantification, and precision dominates the other three perspectives, effectively reducing them to perspective 1. For example, (1) *homo sapiens* is reduced to *homo economicus*;[15] (2) the vast array of human emotions is reduced to a small base of human emotions—fear, greed, trust, and uncertainty;[16] (3) all human motivation is reduced to self-interest;[17] (4) all available information about the economy, industries, firms, and so on is reduced to market prices;[18] and (5) all kinds of risks are reduced to market price volatility and correlations among market prices.[19]

One of the most important manifestations of the EFDs' obsession with reductionism can be seen in how the concept of risk has been treated. For EFDs, risk had been a difficult concept to model and measure until it was reduced and equated to the volatility of market prices.[20] Since then, risk has been often conceptualized as the amount of fluctuations in the value of an investment portfolio (equities, bonds, real estate, and so on) and the extent to which different components of a portfolio move together in value. Risk was no longer an immeasurable, vague concept; it now could be measured quantitatively by using math and statistics. Risk was reduced to a single number.

Such sweeping reductions came with a bunch of assumptions about human nature, the markets, and other subjects. *But in the process of making questionable assumptions, EFDs made their assumptions unquestionable.*[21] When their assumptions were questioned and disconfirming evidence against their assumptions was presented, most EFDs tended to ignore them.[22] Milton Friedman went so far as to say that assumptions behind a model did not matter as long as the model had high predictive power.[23] This is not only a silly argument because prediction without explanation is voodoo science, it is also unethical because the assumptions behind a model (Friedman wrote: "[Economics] assumes man to be selfish and money-grubbing"[24]) affect all of us, particularly if what we are taught in economics becomes self-fulfilling prophecies.[25]

When a set of assumptions are held by a large group of academics (including Nobel Prize winners), and the members of the group control what gets published in journals such as the *Journal of Finance*, then it becomes extremely difficult to question the status quo because doing so lowers one's chances of getting published in top journals (a uniquely perspective 1 criterion for academic tenure) and hence of achieving tenure.

The preceding two paragraphs highlight an important aspect of the current financial mega-mess: it is deeply connected with the tenure system in academic institutions (which is itself a "mess") and cannot be understood fully without at least considering how the culture of academia (perspective 4) contributed to the financial mess. Put differently, the EFDs not only reduce other perspectives to perspective 1, they seem to be oblivious to (or they don't care about) the fact that their very own biases (perspective 3) and culture (perspective 4) contribute to their obliviousness (or lack of caring).

In sum, the reductionist ideas of economics and finance scholars turned previously immeasurable aspects of markets and risk into inaccurate but precisely measurable quantities. These developments, however and unfortunately, did not remain within academic circles. Wall Street eventually realized that it could make a lot of money by selling financial instruments that quantified and measured risk, portfolio diversification, performance of a money manager, and so on.

Wall Street's Culture of Risk

The trading desks on Wall Street could not care less about the definition of risk held by academics. In fact, Wall Street quickly learned that academics' definition of risk, which is based on at least two flawed assumptions, that the future is going to be like today and that investors are rational and independent minded, was a sure recipe for losing money.[26] A case in point is the collapse and bailout of Long-Term Capital Management, a hedge fund that lost about $4 billion in a short amount of time, and whose board of directors featured Nobel Prize recipients Myron Scholes and Robert C. Merton.[27] Nonetheless, Wall Street also figured out that academics' risk formulas and Nobel Prizes, although inaccurate, were useful to the extent they helped legitimate and sell Wall Street's financial innovations to the rest of the world. In fairness, academics warned Wall Street that the risk formulas they used were not accurate, but too late; Wall Street did not fully understand and did not want to understand the risk of not measuring risk accurately.[28] It was too busy making loads of money to care.

In time, the financial innovations or products (such as index funds, ETFs, derivatives, securitization, collateralized debt obligations, and collateralized mortgage obligations) became more and more complex. These products were sold to parties who repackaged and resold them to others, spreading risk while at the same time increasing the correlation between different markets and asset classes. While risk was spread around the world, Wall Street companies' profits and stock prices soared. Leverage was the name of the game. The financial leverage of Goldman Sachs in 2007 before the markets turned south was 28x. Morgan Stanley's financial leverage was even higher: 35x.[29] A 35x leverage means that Morgan Stanley borrowed $35 for every $1 it put at risk. Compare these ratios to Johnson & Johnson's at 1.9x or Apple's at 1.75x.[30]

Risk is not only a formula or a number on Wall Street. It is a way of living, of being. It is a significant aspect of the culture, as we discussed in Chapter 5.

A Bigger Picture

Neither Wall Street nor the economics and finance departments accomplished all of this in a vacuum. To better understand the context, we need to take a different perspective, a sociological one that views what happened in EFDs and Wall Street as one aspect of a broader movement that may be best described as a transition from an industrial society to a postindustrial society.[31] According to Professor Gerald Davis of the University of Michigan, this transition took place over the past thirty years and resulted in the following changes:[32]

1. Service jobs replaced manufacturing jobs; Wal-Mart-like companies replaced GM- and GE-like companies as the largest employer.

2. Temporary employment relations replaced long-term employment relations; employees' investment in firm-specific skills decreased and employee mobility increased.

3. Employers began to offer more portable retirement plans in case an employee changes jobs; individually owned pensions, 401(k)s, and "defined contribution" plans replaced "defined benefit" plans, effectively shifting risk from employers to employees; and employees' fortunes became more independent of their employers' but more dependent on the ups and downs of the financial markets.

4. Employees, not knowing how to invest properly themselves, did not want to take risks and began to invest their savings in mutual funds; as a result of this large inflow of savings, the mutual fund industry prospered; financial intermediaries such as Fidelity and Vanguard became major owners of American corporations.

5. The famous "separation of ownership and control,"[33] which started in the 1920s, was replaced by "re-concentration of ownership and control" in the hands of the finance industry or what is generally known as Wall Street; long-term stockholder

value creation or "shareholder value maximization" became the most important corporate objective;[34] share price became the most relevant measure of corporate performance; and share price volatility became the new measure of risk on Wall Street.

6. Maximizing share price meant "earn the most profits with the least assets"; to do so, corporations in most industries outsourced the activities (such as parts of manufacturing, IT, and HR) that were outside of their core competence; banks and other financial institutions (in other words, Wall Street), however, did something else to free up funds for more lending and to leverage their assets: they began to "securitize," that is, turn any income stream on balance sheets (such as auto loans, home mortgages, or in general almost any accounts receivable) into securities that could be sold to investors and traded on markets.

7. While the ownership of corporations reconcentrated in the hands of the finance industry, "securitization" made possible the dispersing of the ownership of mortgages (and thus risk) among investors around the world, and at the same time, reduced the cost of credit and increased the ease of refinancing; this change, in turn, fueled the U.S. housing bubble, during which homeowners, encouraged by the constant increase in home prices, low interest rates, and the increasing availability of financial products (adjustable rate mortgages, CDOs, and so on), learned to use their homes as ATMs, drawing out $800 billion a year,[35] and without really knowing the amount of risk they were taking.

8. When the unsustainable rise in home prices stopped and reversed, overleveraged financial institutions and consumers suffered major setbacks, sending the economy into a major recession.

The financial crisis of 2008 was one of the results of a significant transition that has been taking place since the 1980s. During this transition, consumer spending became the main driver of U.S.

economic growth, and the U.S. economy became a postindustrial economy. The organizing principles and metaphors of society have changed. "Investor-trader" became the new metaphor for the social agent or actor, and replaced "the organization man," the old metaphor. Similarly, "the ascendance of finance," the new organizing principle or structural metaphor for society, ended the reign of "the society of organizations," the old metaphor.[36]

In sum, it is within this context that finance and economics departments became more prominent and Wall Street prospered. And it is also within this context that global markets became highly complex and tightly coupled, and the financial derivatives and products "manufactured" by Wall Street to reduce risk created even more and unforeseen risks, and eventually put us all at risk.

THE PENDULUM

The argument summarized in the previous section covers the transition from the industrial society to the postindustrial society. It focuses mostly on the characteristics of the period that started with the Great Depression ("the society of organizations") and compares it to the one that started in the 1980s ("the ascent of finance").[37] But this transition is also embedded in a related and larger set of political forces, and a political economics perspective can help us understand certain aspects of it. Specifically, what took place since the 1980s can be seen as the continuation of a more than century-long debate about the best way to increase the economic welfare of societies. This debate can be viewed in terms of pendulums that swing between two extremes:

- Central planning of economic activity by governments *and* allocation of economic resources by market forces

- Keynesian economics *and* Hayekian economics

- Socialism *and* capitalism

- The bureaucrat *and* the entrepreneur

- Collectivism *and* individualism

- The risk of totalitarianism *and* the risk of bubbles or excesses of the market economy.[38]

The "ascent of finance" and the stock market crashes of 2000 and 2008 resemble (but only resemble) the roaring stock market of the 1920s and the crash of 1929. Why only resemble? The pendulum metaphor is limited because each swing (for example, from central planning to market economy and back) is different from the previous swings. Each swing takes place in the context of previous swings. In other words, contexts—our institutions, organizations, technologies, values, beliefs, and the nature of risks we take—change constantly with each swing.

But the pendulum metaphor also highlights the fact that societies commit similar mistakes over and over again: financial crises have been with us for a very long time. In fact, economic historians tell us that financial crises are perennial.[39] They occur regularly. Moreover, the study of financial crises or speculative bubbles is perhaps one of the most conventional topics in economics.[40] Nonetheless, as Robert Shiller argues, we still do not understand or know how to manage speculative bubbles.[41] But why not? Of course, answers to this question cannot be found only within the field of political economy. We need other perspectives to help us.

A Deeper View

A partial answer is the following: the mainstream theories of economics focus almost exclusively on the upper quadrants of the Myers-Briggs framework, and ignore the deeply human side of economics, that is, the lower quadrants of the framework. And we cannot truly understand risk if we ignore the social, cultural, and human sides of risk. As Akerlof and Shiller put it, "To understand how economies work, and how we can manage them and prosper, we must pay attention to the thought patterns that animate people's ideas and feelings, their *animal spirits*."[42]

According to Akerlof and Shiller, the current financial crisis cannot be understood without taking into account the following five aspects of our human and social nature (in other words, the lower two quadrants in our framework):

- *Confidence*: We are not always rational. And we often suspend rationality and skepticism in order to trust. We often make decisions that feel right.

- *Fairness*: Our concern over fairness often overrides our rational economic motivations.

- *Corruption and bad faith*: The prominence and acceptability of such behaviors vary over time, and sometimes for many people the lowering of one's moral standards seems like a perfectly rational decision.

- *Money illusion*: We base our economic decisions on nominal dollar amounts, which is irrational, and not on relative dollar values.

- *Stories*: We use stories and storytelling to make sense of the world. And stories such as those about people making a fortune during the California Gold Rush or the Internet Bubble or the Housing Bubble, in turn, make us and the economy.

Our perceptions of risk and the riskiness of our behavior are shaped not by "rationality" but by our cognitive limits, not by our economic motivations but by our concerns over fairness, not by our predictions about the future but by our confidence in it, and not by "objective" economic facts but by our stories about the facts.

STORIES

It is not the so-called "objective" economic facts that make possible the widespread diffusion and adoption of a particular definition of risk. Rather, it is the persuasiveness of the underlying "stories" (that it is a Nobel Prize–winning idea, that it is parsimonious, quantifiable, and scientific). What makes a person buy a house at the peak of a housing bubble is not the "real" economic or investment value of the house but the persuasiveness of the underlying story (that "home prices always go up," that "everyone is making a profit flipping houses"). Thus a rhetorical analysis of the persuasiveness of the stories tells us a great deal about why and how bubbles and busts, and manias and crashes, occur, and why certain ideas such as "risk as price volatility" diffuse faster than others.

Rhetorical theory provides a great many frameworks to analyze why some stories are more persuasive than others. One of the most robust frameworks is Aristotle's "three appeals": pathos, logos, and ethos.[43] These three have different persuasive powers. Pathos persuades by eliciting emotional responses; ethos persuades by appealing to social mores and values; and logos persuades by appealing to the instrumental, analyzing mind.[44]

The use of pathos, logos, and ethos can be observed, for instance, in the ways the media tell stories to engage and persuade their audience. For instance, when reporting about the financial crisis or the bursting of the housing bubble, pathos focuses on a specific family's loss of savings and their foreclosed home. Logos focuses attention on statistics, such as how many families are reported to have experienced similar problems or the increasing rate of foreclosed homes. Ethos draws on the expertise and trustworthiness of credible sources, such as government officials or academicians, or the values of the community, in order to judge the morals of those who may be responsible for the financial crisis and the housing bust. People respond to stories and the ways stories are told, and the media know this very well.

Rhetorical theory can advance our understanding of financial crises in numerous ways.[45] For instance, rhetoricians have argued that the diffusion and widespread adoption of certain ideas and practices are most effective when they follow a particular rhetorical sequence: pathos, logos, and ethos.[46] Specifically, if the diffusion process of a social practice follows the rhetorical sequence of pathos (initial), logos (middle), and ethos (end), then the practice will be adopted quickly, diffused broadly, and abandoned slowly.[47] In the context of the housing bubble, the rhetorical sequence suggests that appeals to pathos may capture one's attention initially, such that not buying a home sounds like a highly risky investment decision (*"Everyone* is flipping homes to make a profit!" "My uncle in real estate *doubled* his investments in *less* than a year!"). Investors may begin to feel that they are missing out on good investment opportunities, and that the risk of investing in real estate is much less than the risk of being left behind.[48] Appeals to logos may provide further justifications that buying a home leads to more efficient and effective outcomes ("home prices always go up," "land always has value," "a second home is your best investment"). Note that whether these justifications are right or wrong is not the point. What matters is the form and persuasiveness of the argument that "if A then B." Finally, appeals to ethos can reinforce not only that investing in real estate leads to good outcomes for the individual but that it has always been the socially right thing to do ("If you own something, you have a vital stake in the future of our country. The more ownership there is in America, the more vitality there is in America, and the more people have a vital stake in the future of this country."—President George W. Bush, June 17, 2004).

Of course, when no one else is left to be persuaded, when there is no one else to invest in real estate, when the stories lose their "appeal," then they are abandoned and replaced by new ones. Home prices start going down drastically. And thus begins a new episode of storytelling.

Language and rhetoric, the way we talk about things, and the way we tell stories matter. Not only can rhetorical theory help us understand how we construct "risk" in our stories (for example, "it is different this time"), it also can provide insights into the various human causes of financial crises.[49]

CONCLUDING REMARKS

The primary purpose of this chapter has been to use a messy inquiry methodology to provide insights into the current financial crisis. We started with an inquiry into academia. We focused on the role of economics and finance departments as prime contributors to the financial crisis. We argued that most EFDs prefer an extremely technical and narrow approach to the study of economics. In the process

of modeling only that which can be modeled quantitatively and assuming away many of the problems associated with their models,
the EFDs developed a culture that rewards (by tenure, Nobel prizes,
and A-list journal publications) only a narrow approach to the study
of risk in particular and of economics in general. In effect, they not
only failed to model risk properly, they also created and believed
in the illusion that they understand risk when in fact they don't. In
short, they solved the wrong problem precisely. This only added to
the overall risk because, as Warren Buffett says, "Risk comes from
not knowing what you are doing."

The main point here is not that the EFDs are the sole or primary
cause of the financial crisis, but that they are a significant part of
it, and without understanding the tenure process and the culture of
EFDs, we cannot truly understand the financial crisis.

Next we swept in another influential factor, Wall Street's culture of risk, to provide more insight into the financial crisis. We
discussed extensively the culture of Wall Street in Chapter 5. But it
is important to repeat that Wall Street took what EFDs had to offer
and ran with it, creating more and more complex financial products
that were built on false assumptions.

Next we swept in a sociological perspective to understand what
made it possible for Wall Street and EFDs to become influential.
Both EFDs and Wall Street were parts of a larger system and culture, and they became more prominent as a result of the shift from
an industrial society to a postindustrial society. In economics terms,
the demand for the services Wall Street and EFDs offered to society increased as the United States became a more service-oriented
economy in the past thirty years. As the organizing metaphors and
structures of society have changed, so have the complexity and interconnectedness of economic transactions and hence the nature of risk.

Next we swept in a political perspective. We argued that the shift
that occurred in the past thirty years is in fact part of a set of swings
between two distinctive approaches to increasing the economic welfare of societies. We argued that in order to understand the current
crisis, we need to understand the historical tensions between two

extremes such as capitalism and socialism, individualism and collectivism, and so on. Both extremes contain the seeds of their own destruction (fourth way of knowing), and in the process of becoming more extreme, they create their own demise in the form of bubbles, busts, and the like. In other words, economic or financial crises occur all the time, whether as a result of capitalism or socialism or any economic system taken too far. This raises a deceptively simple question: What is common and somewhat invariant to all of these swings, booms and busts, and manias and crashes? One answer is our incomplete understanding of human nature and risk. We next swept in behavioral economics (perspectives 3 and 4) and argued that our human and social natures are integral parts of our financial systems and must be understood properly to avoid financial crises.

Finally, we swept in a rhetorical perspective. We argued that if stories are the basic things that move us, then analyzing and understanding how the language and rhetoric of stories create and shape our risk perceptions may provide another missing piece of the puzzle of financial crises.

We could sweep in many more disciplines and perspectives to improve our understanding. By no means would the factors above prevent the next financial crisis. But excluding them and other disciplines would contribute to the next financial crisis.

In the following chapter, we apply some of the ideas discussed in this book to the financial sector.

9   T R U S T ,   T R A N S P A R E N C Y ,

A N D   R E L I A B I L I T Y

What Can the HROs Teach the Financial Sector?

THIS CHAPTER EXAMINES the financial sector in greater detail than was done in previous chapters so that it can then be looked at from the standpoint of high reliability organizations (HROs). The major question is, "What do HROs have to teach the financial sector so that we can lower the chances of catastrophic failures even if we cannot fully prevent them?" The chapter not only applies some of the lessons that have been learned from HROs in particular and crisis management in general, it also examines the role of mistaken beliefs, false assumptions, and trust in financial systems. It outlines as well four essential trust-enhancing elements for a high reliability financial sector.

The chapter also examines a particular and unorthodox, but nonetheless doable, way of insuring organizations against future crises within their industry. It does this by combining a number of dissimilar and unconventional ideas and mechanisms. For instance, it uses in a novel way one of the prime mechanisms that got us into the financial crisis. In other words, it uses a particular financial mechanism to protect organizations from the financial aspects of major crises. It thus has special appeal to those who are motivated primarily by cost-to-benefit arguments as to whether to prepare or not to prepare for major crises.

WHAT IS A "HIGH RELIABILITY ORGANIZATION"?

We have already stated in Chapter 7 that the concept of high reliability organizations has been used to understand and design organizations (such as nuclear power plants, air traffic controllers, offshore oil rigs, or electric power plants) whose technologies are so critical that if they fail then huge and terrible consequences will result. But we have not provided much detail as to how they accomplish it.

To understand the concept of HROs, one must understand the concept of "normal accidents," which was first introduced by Charles Perrow in 1984, after having studied the Three Mile Island nuclear power plant incident.[1] According to Perrow, some accidents are "normal" in the sense that, when the conditions are right, they are inevitable. The two conditions are "complex interactions" and "tight coupling."

Systems interactions are complex if the components can interact in unfamiliar, unplanned, and unexpected ways, or if the interactions are either invisible or incomprehensible.[2] A system is tightly coupled if the components are so interdependent that if one of them fails, other components are quickly affected.[3]

The main practical implication of Perrow's theory is this: if a system is characterized by highly complex interactions and tight coupling, then reducing the level of complexity and the tightness of coupling in the system may help it avoid "normal" accidents.[4] Clearly there are many types of organizations, such as hospitals, chemical refineries, aircraft carriers, nuclear power plants, and metropolitan subway systems, that can benefit from Perrow's insights. But how these organizations can and should reduce system complexity and decouple system components is not a trivial matter, and has prompted numerous studies.[5] Indeed, scholars have studied some of these organizations that were supposed to fail but didn't to see why and how they were able to minimize the severity and frequency of the accidents they experienced.[6]

WHAT WOULD A HIGH RELIABILITY
FINANCIAL SECTOR LOOK LIKE?

Put simply, the financial sector is like the circulatory system of the human body. It circulates money and credit, without which no economy could function, and like the circulatory system, if it fails, its failure is catastrophic and may trigger not only economic recessions and depressions but the collapse of the social fabric as well.

The financial sector's reliable intermediation of money flow is vital to an economy's long-term growth, stability, and healthy functioning. This intermediation is so basic that without it the conduct of business is extremely difficult, if not virtually impossible. Companies or countries that do not have access to world financial markets, and hence to credit at competitive rates, are at a disadvantage unless they are able to finance themselves.

Given the financial sector's role in facilitating business around the globe, it should come as no surprise (in fact, one must consider this an early warning signal) that it has grown to become the largest sector in the U.S. economy, making up more than 20 percent of the S&P 500 index in 2007.[7] It has also become extremely connected with all of the other sectors in the global economy. The size of the financial sector, its role in facilitating global business, and its connections to other sectors highlight the importance of its being properly regulated and run.

The global financial system is at least as tightly coupled and complex as a nuclear power plant. In fact, the financial system is probably more tightly coupled because it was not explicitly designed to reduce its coupling; instead, as it has evolved, its coupling increased along with the accelerating pace of globalization. But not everyone thinks that tight coupling and complexity are all that bad. In fact, some scholars believe that complexity and tight coupling are desirable attributes of a financial system. These attributes, at least in theory, make markets more efficient: complex financial instruments (such as derivatives, SIVs, CDOs, CDSs, and MBSs) make different ways of investing and hedging possible, and

the tight coupling of all financial systems removes arbitrage opportunities from the markets very quickly. Other scholars believe
that this is a contentious claim and that while complex financial
tools may help lower an individual investor's risk, complex interactions between different financial instruments can increase the
risk to the overall system.[8]

The enormous complexity and the tight coupling of the global
financial system can be easily observed in financial markets around
the world. Price movements in these markets, especially nowadays,
are increasingly and strongly correlated. At the push of a button, economic news about countries or companies and billions of investment
dollars travel around the world in milliseconds. Computers execut-
ing complex algorithms make most of the trades. High-frequency,
high-speed trading by computers on electronic exchanges has replaced the floor traders. More than a thousand exchange-traded
funds (ETFs) and other financial tools allow investors to diversify,
focus, and hedge their investments in any way they like.

But complexity and tight coupling sometimes prove costly. When
big mistakes are made, they are amplified very quickly. For instance,
on May 6, 2010, during the writing of this book, the stock markets, unexpectedly and for no immediately visible or comprehensible
reason, crashed and recovered nearly 10 percent in a few minutes
(share prices of some companies dropped to $0.01 per share), caus-
ing traders to stop trusting the numbers they saw on their screens
and scaring away many individual investors, particularly those who
lost a lot of money as a result of the sudden drop.

At least for the reasons identified above and because of its critical intermediating role in the global economy, the financial system
must operate in as close to an error-free manner as possible; it must
operate like an HRO. In fact, there are already rules and regulations
to decrease the degree of complexity and coupling in the financial
system. For example, the stock exchanges have a number of circuit
breakers—trading halt rules, trading price limits, margin require-
ments, and the like—to maintain the reliability of the system.

But when the financial system is considered as a whole, satisfying the two conditions of high reliability (less complexity and loose coupling) is by itself not sufficient. For it does not take fully into account the "performative" nature of finance and economics: that they create the phenomena they describe.[9] For example, believing that the Black-Scholes option-pricing formula works makes it work:[10] teaching that individuals seek self-interest creates such individuals.[11]

In contrast to the conditions of complexity and tight coupling, which emphasize the technical, structural, organizational, and relatively shorter term aspects of financial systems, the property of "performativity" has more to do with the social, psychological, ethical, and both short- and long-term aspects of financial systems.

An important implication of performativity for the financial systems is that false assumptions and mistaken beliefs held about things can create and shape, for a very long time, the very things to which they refer. In other words, financial systems are prone to self-reinforcing trends that are unsustainable in the long run (such as bubbles and busts), and self-fulfilling prophecies that eventually prove to be wrong (for example, the efficient market hypothesis and the Black-Scholes option-pricing formula).[12] Consider a concrete example: a belief among depositors that a bank will go bankrupt can cause a run on the bank and force the bank to go bankrupt, regardless of the bank's true financial health.

Consider also the effect of performativity on market price volatility. Studies have suggested that the level of volatility in market prices is too high to be explained solely by investors' responses to world events (such as changes in economic trends or changes in firm prospects) or mistakes investors make.[13] A great deal of the volatility in the markets, however, can be explained by the reaction of current market prices to past market prices.[14] Given the practice of defining and measuring risk in terms of price volatility, the performative effect of market price volatility is not surprising.

Notice that some forms of performativity such as self-fulfilling prophecies may not be observed in other HROs as often as they are observed in the financial systems. Mistaken assumptions about, say, the chemical properties of a metal rod may trigger an accident but they do not change temporarily the "real" properties of the metal.

As we argued in Chapter 8, not many scholarly studies of HROs have looked beyond complex interactions and tight coupling to include in their analyses the role of performativity and trust, both of which are critical in understanding how the financial system works. To account for the financial system's vulnerability to the issues of performativity and loss of trust, the conditions of high reliability need to be broadened.

The Myers-Briggs framework in Figure 9.1 presents a visual representation of a broader view of high reliability. This view takes into account the issues of performativity and loss of trust in the financial systems. The main practical implication is clear: lowering the negative effects of performativity and increasing the level of trust in the financial systems may help them avoid not only "normal" (unintentional) accidents but also "abnormal" (intentional) crises.[15]

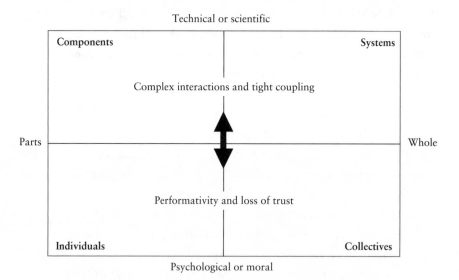

FIGURE 9.1.   A broader view of high reliability

FOUR ESSENTIAL ELEMENTS

A high reliability and trust-enhancing financial sector requires four essential elements to deal with the negative effects of performativity and loss of trust before they lead to a full-blown financial mega-crisis:

1. Recognizing the importance of detecting early warning signals

2. Constantly bringing to the surface and critiquing taken-for-granted assumptions

3. Unwavering support for simplicity

4. Deep respect and support for regulations and transparency

Detection of Early Warning Signals

A highly reliable financial system must be able to detect and act upon the early warning signals of a crisis, which may include, among many others, unsustainable trends and self-fulfilling prophecies. Early detection is critical because once a financial mega-crisis begins to unfold, there usually is no easy way to stop it or contain its damage.

The 1997 Asian financial crisis and the current financial crisis share a remarkably similar set of early warning signals of unsustainable trends: (1) lax credit standards that allowed investors to borrow at low interest rates; (2) massive inflows of capital that led to a rise in lending and borrowing; (3) an aggressive search for higher returns on investment, which fueled the demand for highly leveraged financial instruments such as collateralized debt obligations (CDOs); and (4) rapid price increases in equity markets and property values both in Asia and the United States.[16] An effective signal detection mechanism for the financial sector must pick up a wide variety of early warning signals and would have also picked up some or all of the following early warning signals of the current crisis: too many homebuyers who borrowed too much to buy or "flip" a house they could not afford; mortgage brokers who deceived borrowers into taking out NINJA loans (no income, no job or asset); and increasingly more undecipherable and complex financial instruments used to securitize, repackage, and sell these loans.

Scanning for early warning is a necessary but insufficient condition of a high reliability financial system. Financial institutions, organizations, and regulatory agencies need a central location where different signals can be connected to see the big picture or the whole problem. The signals must also be acted upon. Thus they must first be transmitted by the right people in the right form to the right people or groups within the system. To do so, the financial system as a whole must embrace the detection of early warning signals as an integral and indispensable aspect of its culture, organizational structures, and reward systems.

Unfortunately, early signal detection has not often been the highest priority of financial institutions and regulatory agencies. Bernie Madoff, who had been running the largest Ponzi scheme in history, was not caught until he turned himself in. The early warning signals of his scheme were not picked up and acted upon by the authorities. In fact, a financial fraud investigator, Harry Markopoulos, had warned the U.S. Securities Exchange Commission (SEC) several times about Madoff.[17] Markopoulos had even explained to the SEC how Madoff swindled his investors. Unfortunately, the SEC did not amplify these signals, act upon them, or transmit them to the right people.

To summarize, a high reliability financial system must satisfy at least four conditions in order to be able to detect bubbles and busts, manias and panics, and Ponzi schemes long before they happen: (1) early warning signal detectors and monitors that are designed and put in place long before a crisis occurs, (2) an ability and willingness to recognize a wide range of signals, (3) a culture that can piece together a wide variety of signals into a larger pattern, and (4) a culture that does not block signals but rather amplifies them.[18]

Assumption Surfacing and Testing

Members of the financial sector must develop a sense for events that are out of the ordinary, or "abnormal." To do so, they must constantly question their assumptions about what is "normal." They must always be concerned with the validity of their assumptions. The property of performativity implies that, in the context of the financial system, assumptions can create and shape the world until they prove to be wrong.

A powerful example of mistaken assumptions is the collapse of Long-Term Capital Management (LTCM), a hedge fund started in 1994. In 1998, LTCM single-handedly threatened to bring down the whole financial system when it was caught on the wrong side of a trade. Why? Because the fund managers at LTCM mistakenly assumed that the chance of the Russian government defaulting on its debt was extremely low.

The financial models used at LTCM were based on the mistaken assumption that changes in asset prices are normally distributed, and that the Russian government defaulting on their bonds was a one-in-a-billion-chance event. Because this event was considered to be extremely improbable and because LTCM's bets were big and extremely leveraged, increasing the tightness of coupling between LTCM and other financial institutions, its failure threatened to collapse the whole financial system.

The collapse and bailout of LTCM was also one of the early warning signals of the current crisis. LTCM's bailout by other banks provided a powerful example of how "too big to fail" worked in practice. In effect, it signaled to Wall Street that a financial institution would be bailed out if it threatened to collapse the whole financial system.

The option-pricing model (the One True Formula!) originated by Fisher Black and Nobel laureates Myron Scholes and Robert C. Merton, who served on LTCM's board of directors, shaped the very way investors talked about and priced options. The model was performative. But most people may not know that when it was first formulated, not only were the option-pricing model's assumptions very unrealistic, the actual prices of options were very different from those that the model predicted.[19] Over time, thanks to the efforts of many individuals and institutions, the pricing of options changed to fit the model's predictions. That is, instead of the model merely reflecting reality, reality came to fit the model! The model was accepted and thought to be an ordinary financial tool used by investors and financial institutions (Expert Consensus!).

Madoff's ability to swindle investors out of billions of dollars is another powerful example of unquestioned assumptions. Madoff was able to operate and hide in plain sight because people trusted him. People assumed that they could trust Madoff because: (1) he had been in business and successful for a very long time; (2) he was an "expert"; (3) he had served as head of NASDAQ; (4) he had been secretive because he had a working, proprietary formula for investing; (5) he had refused to work with a well-established accounting firm because he was trying to protect his formula; (6) royalty and those who were rich from all around the world also trusted Madoff with their investments.

The examples of LTCM and Madoff indicate that the financial system must constantly question its assumptions. A concern with assumptions and a skeptical attitude toward the normal is not only extremely important in systems designed to run reliably, it is also instrumental in spotting black swans: large-impact, hard-to-predict events.[20] Those in a financial system must develop the skills required to escape their mental and emotional blinders and to question their own assumptions as strongly as necessary while at the same time trying to avoid dysfunctional behavior associated with being gullible or too skeptical (see Chapter 6). This "essential tension" is an old one and requires that financial institutions be comfortable navigating the extremes of total devotion and total acceptance, tradition and change, and cautiousness and curiosity. In short, they must be able to use the fourth way of knowing (see Chapter 7) and operate at the highest possible levels of awareness.

As Simple as Possible but Not Simpler

Einstein once said, "Everything should be made as simple as possible, but not simpler." Too many of today's financial instruments are designed by people with PhDs in mathematics and physics. Thus they are too complex for most others to understand. Nonetheless, people who cannot calculate one percent of one thousand are expected to decipher adjustable rate mortgage rates, negative amortizations, and other new tools of the trade. Even regulators have struggled to decipher all the intricacies of Wall Street's models of risk and valuation. Alan Greenspan admitted on national television that he didn't fully understand collateralized debt obligations (a type of investment vehicle in which value and payments are derived from a portfolio of fixed-income assets such as home mortgages). No one, not even the creators of these financial instruments, could fully understand their effects. Warren Buffett had a good reason for referring to them as "financial weapons of mass destruction."

The current risk and econometric models are indeed extremely complex for many of us. But according to Professor Shiller, they are also too simple to capture the complexities of the economic realities they try to model.[21] We agree. In fact, we believe that they are more than simple: they are reductionist. As we have discussed in the previous chapter in more detail, these models ignore the human and social aspects of economic activity and reduce the complexities of markets and economies to a set of numbers (One True Formula!). Unless these ignored aspects can be modeled with sufficient sophistication, the complexity of risk and econometric models must be kept at a reasonable level. In other words, financial and economic models that are based on simplistic assumptions and complex mathematical formulas must be replaced by models that are based on sophisticated assumptions and mathematical formulas that are no more complex than the assumptions on which they are based.

To counteract the tendency of financial instruments to become increasingly more complex and unsustainable (for it is impossible to leverage returns and spread risks forever), a highly reliable financial sector must do everything in its power to reduce complexity and make financial instruments understandable to everyone involved.

An unwavering support and demand for simplicity will make financial products more transparent and comprehensible; interactions between borrowers and lenders more manageable and less costly; government regulations more effective and enforceable; and outliers, early warning signals, unsustainable trends, and wrong assumptions more easily detectable. More important, simpler financial tools will keep leverage at sustainable levels, creating a buffer zone between financial markets and the real economy. Finally, simpler financial tools will not allow financial institutions to blame complexity and to avoid moral responsibility for the systems they have created. In short, it is hoped that simpler financial tools and more sophisticated assumptions will increase the trust of stakeholders in the financial system, and hence its reliability as well as sustainability.

Respect and Support for Regulations and Transparency

One of the best examples of a critical threat to the global financial system was the credit default swap (CDS) market, which dates back to the 1990s. The CDS market was estimated at $62 trillion in 2007. To put this number in perspective, it was about 90 percent of the world GDP, or three times the U.S. GDP.

A credit default swap is basically an unregulated insurance policy that anyone can take out on any company. Essentially a CDS is a bet that if a company fails, then the insurance policy will pay off the owner of the policy. The buyers of the policy are not regulated. Thus anyone, regardless of whether they have something that can be insured or not, can take out a CDS on any company as long as there is a seller. And they can do it as many times as they want.

The sellers are not regulated either. The sellers of CDSs do not have to have enough money in reserve to pay off the buyers of CDSs if the insured company defaults on its debt. Furthermore, there is no regulation that ensures that the buyers cannot turn around and sell the same CDS to other buyers. In short, there is almost nothing that prevents buyers and sellers from engaging in leveraged and un-limited amounts of CDS transactions. The lack of regulation partly explains why the CDS market has grown from $1 trillion to $62 trillion in ten years. There is also no transparency. It is very difficult to know whether a buyer of a CDS will get paid should the insured company go bust. In fact, given the size of the CDS market and the complex, tightly coupled chains of CDS transactions among financial institutions, there is a significant chance that a sharp drop in inves-tors' trust in the ability of the sellers to pay may easily threaten to collapse the global financial system. We witnessed this near collapse when companies that were assumed to have a low probability of going bust, such as AIG, were all of a sudden at the brink of bankruptcy, threatening to take down the financial system with them. Note that sometimes the loss of trust in these companies and the resulting belief that these companies will go bust may cause them go bust, just like a run on banks.

Financial markets require transparency. They require that buyers and sellers have access to accurate information that they need to price investments, and that regulators monitor the financial system for fraudulent activity. When either or both of these conditions are invalid, considerable uncertainty can exist about the true value of investments. When the true value of investments is in question, those who hold them may try to get rid of them quickly, creating excessive price volatility and forcing investors to close their positions because they need to pay off their debt, lowering prices across the board. This triggers more selling elsewhere, creating a vicious circle of selling and more selling; a lack of trust among buyers and sellers; a massive freeze in financial markets; and, in the absence of appropriate government intervention, an eventual meltdown of the global financial system.

To achieve the level of reliability the global financial system requires, all of the stakeholders must be willing to create and follow regulations that focus on fairness, accuracy, and transparency; monitor their enforcement; and allocate adequate resources so that the regulations can be constantly and appropriately adjusted. Financial organizations and institutions must not only respect existing regulations but also do everything in their power to increase the effectiveness of regulators.

The state of regulatory agencies today is unfortunately far from optimum. Some scholars question the culture and practices of monitoring agencies such as the SEC, and argue that regulators had the authority to restrain fraudulent practices but did not use their authority. For example, the SEC failed to catch Bernie Madoff, although his Ponzi scheme was easy to detect and did not require a great deal of manpower or resources.

Regulators have also failed to monitor the greedy, misunderstood, and sometimes criminal lending practices such as no document loans and liar's loans. Other scholars have pointed out that regulators were not able to perform effectively because they lacked sufficient resources. For example, whereas almost everyone on Wall Street has access to a Bloomberg Terminal, a subscription-based service that provides real-time access to news, financial market data, and so on, the ratio is much lower at the Securities Exchange Commission. Regulators cannot succeed if they are using sticks and stones to fight against the financial weapons of mass destruction.

An appropriately regulated financial system is more transparent, making fraudulent activity and outliers more easily detectable and financial institutions more accountable. It also does not allow leverage (in other words, borrowing in order to improve returns on investment) to increase beyond a sustainable level. Nor does it allow the operation of the so-called shadow banking system of non-bank highly leveraged institutions that intermediate between lenders and borrowers but without the same regulations as depository banks.[22]

In sum, in a highly reliable and transparent financial sector, regulators must have the will and the basic ability to monitor market activity, the flexibility to adjust regulations appropriately, and the power to enforce regulations strictly.

We cannot afford *not* to operate a financial system as an HRO. But unless the four trust-enhancing elements just discussed are designed into the financial system, our ability to operate it as an HRO will diminish significantly. Although we are optimistic that the financial sector will one day operate as an HRO, the history of financial crises and our experience with organizations suggest that we are still far from that ideal. Nonetheless, there may be some things organizations can do to protect themselves from major economic crises.

PLAN B: A "NOT SO NICE" WAY OF
INSURING AGAINST FUTURE CRISES

In the absence of a highly reliable financial system, organizations may still try to insure themselves against future crises within their industry. Here is an unorthodox, "not so nice" but doable way of protecting organizations from the economic aspects of major crises:

1. An organization creates an internal assassination team (IAT)[23] that performs a unique vulnerability audit of the organization. By having direct access to the inner workings of the organization, the IAT creates scenarios that can bring the organization to its knees. It thereby identifies a broad array of issues and attempts to fix those that are controllable to the best of their ability. But of course many issues may be uncontrollable.

2. The IAT also assesses the external environment for trends, shocks, early but weak warning signals, and strong but denied warning signals.

3. The IAT creates a list of the organization's competitors and the competitors' vulnerabilities. Gathering and analyzing information about competitors *must* be done in a legal and ethical manner, and may involve examining publicly available corporate announcements, publications, and filings and scanning the environment for competitive corporate actions.

4. The IAT works with different departments such as finance, legal, and risk management to create a hedging strategy to insure the organization against crises. This hedging strategy may involve buying significantly out-of-the-money puts (insurance) on competitors' stocks; buying or selling puts, calls, or futures on certain raw material inputs such as oil, copper, or agricultural commodities; and so on. Note that all of the requisite SEC disclosures must be made properly. Note also that the options, futures, and equity markets are more regulated than the CDS markets.

An Example: The Housing Bubble

Consider the residential home construction industry. Prominent company examples are D.R. Horton, NVR, Standard Pacific, KB Home, Toll Brothers, Lennar, and Pulte Homes.

During the runup in home prices, the executives of these companies were under extreme pressure to produce profits. There was a lot of demand for houses at high prices, so the supply had to go up for them to reap profits. If, say, KB Home had decided not to participate in the "game" or the "bubble," which would have been the right thing to do, its bonuses, stock price, and profits would have suffered because another company would have taken its place.

Given that home construction is a relatively scalable operation, what did KB Home do? Like everyone else, it continued to build new homes.

But there were early warning signs of a potential crisis: Between 1997 and 2006, real home prices in the United States increased by 85 percent, and the economic fundamentals could not justify this increase.[24] Particularly toward the end of 2005, home prices had risen almost 25 percent in two years. It was obvious, at least to industry insiders, that something extraordinary was happening. What was not so obvious was when the increase in home prices would stop and reverse. The signal that home prices could be heading down came around 2005–6, when home prices stopped going up and concerns about subprime lending practices were raised. There were other signals of unsustainable trends as well:

- The runup in commodity prices
- Record low unemployment
- International housing bubbles

A "not so nice" way for KB Home to have operated would have included the following:

1. Create an IAT to perform a vulnerability audit.

2. Collect environmental signals and create future scenarios.

3. Take action and fix problems that could be fixed within the company.

4. Look at competitors and see if they were suffering from the same problems and whether they were doing anything about them.

5. If they were not, then identify those that were vulnerable. (There are very simple things to do such as look at the short-term cash and debt on balance sheets and assess how long these companies can survive if something goes wrong.)

6. Buy significantly out-of-the-money put options (insurance) on vulnerable companies and on certain commodities (such as copper). Not only are the prices of significantly out-of-the-money options extremely low, the value of these options may go up significantly, particularly when the share prices of the underlying assets drop by 80 to 90 percent.

The strategy above tries to guarantee that a company can achieve two conflicting goals:

1. Benefit from some of the upside.

2. Don't get hurt too much by the downside.

How does it work?

KB Home would participate in the upside by competing with construction companies. Its participation would be controlled because the company knows its own vulnerabilities. Perhaps it will say "no" to some of the new construction projects, but not to all of them. On the basis of the company's resources and vulnerabilities, it would pick the better projects in which to engage.

When the top was reached in home prices and new home construction, and the decline began (and no one knew for sure when this would happen), most companies would begin to suffer, including KB Home. But the vulnerable companies (overly leveraged; low on cash; those exposed to California, Florida, Nevada, and Arizona housing markets; and so on) would suffer more. The insurance or the put options would kick in, providing a cushion for KB Home. In fact, KB Home might cover some or all of its losses by these insurance payments either coming from the stock market or some other place. (FYI: The share prices of all of the home builders and other housing-sector-related companies dropped well below their 2005–6 levels. For example, the SPDR S&P Home Builders

Exchange Traded Fund, which includes companies whose earnings are tied to the housing sector, declined more than 60 percent since 2006. Similarly, Lennar declined 95 percent from its all-time highs in mid-2005. Standard Pacific Corporation, one of the more leveraged home builders, declined from its all-time high at around $50 per share in July 2005 to less than $1 per share in March 2009. That is a more than 98 percent drop. During the same time period, KB Home shares declined about 90 percent.)

It wouldn't have made much sense for KB Home to insure itself fully for such a drop because, theoretically, they would have engaged in crisis management activities such as signal detection, scenarios, internal assassin teams, and simulations, and they wouldn't have needed insurance as much as their competitors. Indeed, crisis management would have been their insurance.

One of the key ideas here is that KB Home would have needed to engage in crisis management to really know what their and others' vulnerabilities were. Otherwise, they would have been guessing.

Why is this idea "not-so-nice"?

It seems like KB Home would have been benefiting from others' misfortunes, but think of it this way, using Lennar as an example.

Lennar knows that someone is buying significantly out-of-the-money put options on Lennar. This is information that Lennar can use to reevaluate itself. It's an early warning signal that Lennar's IAT should have picked up. If Lennar gets its act together, KB Home would not want to bet Lennar is going down. The same is true with all of the other organizations in the industry. If they all get their act together then the crisis would not be as bad.

It's difficult to say that the crisis would not have happened, but we believe that it would not have been as bad.

The current system is set up in such a way that the CEOs do not have any incentive to be safe rather than sorry (example: big bailouts and too-big-to-fail arguments). If there is a housing bubble, they will take advantage of it, maximizing their incomes as well as shareholder value, albeit for a limited period. Our "not-so-nice way" offers a way for them to make profits and keep them while avoiding losses. We think they will take it. But here is the catch: if many organizations do take it, then the "not-so-nice way" should stop working because it lessens the impact of the crisis and makes companies more crisis prepared. Which is exactly what we want: a positive form of performativity that makes crisis management more and more attractive!

Of course, we are sure that there are gaps in our "Great Plan of Making Crisis Management Attractive to Corporate America"! But the point is that the chapter offers what we believe is an innovative way to encourage organizations to engage in crisis management.

Managing Crises Proactively Because It's the Right Thing to Do
Make no mistake: we are not advocating that companies should engage in crisis management because it is more profitable to do so. On the contrary, we believe that companies should engage in crisis management because it is the right thing to do. Profits, as Russ Ackoff put it, are never ends in themselves but are means to other ends such as increasing the quality of work life and the standard of living for its stakeholders.

The ends of crisis management are no different. In fact, the primary goal of crisis management is never only to maximize shareholder value or profits; it is always to minimize stakeholder losses.[25] True, managers have a fiduciary duty to the shareholders of the corporation. But, as we explained in Chapter 4, in the context of crises, the duty of stakeholder loss minimization as well as the prima facie duties of reparation, beneficence, and non-maleficence must dominate the duty of shareholder value maximization or the profit motive.

CONCLUDING REMARKS
In this chapter, we raised several questions and made suggestions about how to operate the financial system. While we have applied lessons learned from the HROs to the financial sector, we have also identified a trade-off the financial system has to make, and a fundamental difference between HROs and the financial sector.

The trade-off is between the costs and benefits of complexity and tight coupling. Complexity and tight coupling, the two conditions most HROs try to fix, may be desirable attributes of a financial system because they may make the markets more efficient (benefit). But complexity and tight coupling also increase systemic risk (cost).

The fundamental difference between the HROs and the financial system concerns the concept of "performativity," which is critical to the reliable operations of the financial system. The negative effects of performativity, often observed in the form of self-fulfilling prophecies that eventually prove to be false (such as the efficient market hypothesis, the Black-Scholes option-pricing model, and the rational man model) or in the form of self-reinforcing trends that are unsustainable in the long run (the housing bubbles and busts, extremely low interest rates, stock market bubbles and busts, and so on) can devastate the economy and undermine everyone's trust in the financial system.

We suggested that there are at least four things one can do to make the financial sector more reliable and trust enhancing:

1. Detect early warning signals of unsustainable trends as soon as possible.

2. Acknowledge and question taken-for-granted assumptions.

3. Put sophisticated assumptions and simple math over simplistic assumptions and sophisticated math.

4. Respect and support regulations so as to increase the levels of fairness, accuracy, and transparency in the system.

If history is any guide, financial crises will be with us for a long time. Thus, for those who are motivated by cost-benefit analyses, we outlined a way of insuring and preparing for future financial and economic crises. We believe that those who want to do the right thing have already engaged in proactive crisis management to prepare for a wide variety of crises, including financial and economic.

I T BEHOOVES US to state as succinctly as we can some of the primary conclusions of this book.

1. A mess is a system or complex and dynamically interacting web of ill-defined or wicked problems, conundrums, paradoxes, puzzles, crises, and their solutions, as well as the stated and unstated, conscious and unconscious assumptions, beliefs, emotions, and values that underlie these problems and solutions.

2. A mess is always a part of other messes.

3. All crises are messes. But not all messes are crises. Improperly conceptualized and managed messes turn into crises.

4. Effective management of messes requires high levels of tolerance for messiness, complexity, ambiguity, and uncertainty.

5. Effective management of messes requires high levels of consciousness (that is, advanced stages of human development) or awareness of one's self, others, and the environment.

6. There is a method to the madness of messy inquiry.

   a. Assumptions, not facts, are the fundamental building blocks of reality.

   b. Values, assumptions, theories, and facts are inseparable.

   c. A partially wrong answer to the right question is better than a completely correct answer to the wrong question.

   d. Treating the whole partially is better than treating a part completely.

   e. There is no "basic" discipline, profession, or body of knowledge that is sufficient to define the wickedly complex nature of messes.

   f. All disciplines, professions, and perspectives presuppose each other.

   g. Objectivity is a property shared by inquiring minds and is not a property of a messy situation. Thus there are many types of objectivity.

7. The commonly held belief that there must be a single, universal definition of a crisis is wrong. The definitions and redefinitions of a crisis emerge from one's interactions with it.

8. Because different stakeholders are at different levels of consciousness or awareness (stages of human development), they invariably view crises differently.

9. No two crises are identical. But all crises follow the same general patterns.

   a. Every crisis is human-caused.

   b. Every crisis is a system of multiple crises.

   c. Every crisis involves every known field of inquiry.

   d. Every crisis destroys our assumptions about ourselves, the goodness and the safety of our society, and the world in general.

 e. Every crisis creates a sense of moral outrage.

 f. Every crisis is an existential crisis of meaning.

10. Solving the wrong problems precisely by defining them too narrowly is the first cardinal sin of crisis management. Solving the wrong problems intentionally is the second.

11. There are *no* good rational or ethical reasons for being unprepared for crises.

12. The moral imperative of crisis management is this: expand your awareness and understanding of every system of problems (messes and crises) right up to and as far beyond your comfort zone as you, your organization, and society can tolerate.

Finally, messes encompass the inability to bring to the surface or detect, confront, or stop swans (false assumptions and mistaken beliefs), swine (greed, hubris, arrogance, and narcissism), and swindlers (unethical and corrupt behavior). Indeed, messes are the quintessential combination (system) of swans, swine, and swindlers. They must be managed as such or they cannot be managed at all.

PREFACE

1. Nassim N. Taleb, *The Black Swan: The Impact of the Highly Improbable* (New York: Random House, 2007). We thank Dr. Chris Bresnahan for thinking up the "rhythm of threes" used in the title of this book.

2. See Taleb, *The Black Swan.*

3. Taleb, *The Black Swan.* See also Nouriel Roubini and Stephen Mihm, *Crisis Economics: A Crash Course in the Future of Finance* (n.p.: Penguin Press HC, 2010).

4. Charles P. Kindleberger and Robert Aliber, *Manias, Panics, and Crashes: A History of Financial Crises*, 4th ed. (New York: John Wiley, 2000).

5. "*Deepwater Horizon* Drills World's Deepest Oil & Gas Well," *Transocean,* News and Events 2010, http://www.deepwater.com/fw/main /IDeepwater-Horizon-i-Drills-Worlds-Deepest-Oil-and-Gas-Well-419C151 .html (accessed August 3, 2010).

6. Russell L. Ackoff, *Re-Creating the Corporation* (New York: Oxford University Press, 1999), 324.

7. Ibid., 178–79.

8. Emery Roe, "Mess & Reliability: Reconstructing Policy, Management and Politics," unpublished manuscript, personal communication with Emery Roe.

9. United States General Accounting Office Report to the Chairman,

Subcommittee on Asia and the Pacific, Committee on International Relations, House of Representatives, *Emerging Infectious Diseases, Asian SARS Outbreak Challenged International and National Responses*, GAO-04-564 (Washington, DC: USGAO, April 2004).

10. Karen Ho, *Liquidated: An Ethnography of Wall Street* (Durham, NC: Duke University Press, 2009).

11. Hyman Minsky, "The Financial Instability Hypothesis," working paper #74, the Jerome Levy Economics Institute of Bard College, 1992, 7–8.

12. See Ho, *Liquidated*.

13. Graciela Chichilnisky and Ho-Mou Wu, "General Equilibrium with Endogenous Uncertainty and Default," *Journal of Mathematical Economics* 42 (2006): 499–524.

14. John Cassidy, "Rational Irrationality," *New Yorker*, October 5, 2009, 31.

15. For interdisciplinary, multidisciplinary, and multilevel approaches to crises, see Michael A. Roberto, "Lessons from Everest: The Interaction of Cognitive Bias, Psychological Safety, and System Complexity," *California Management Review* 45, no. 1 (2002): 136–58; Allison Graham, *Essence of Decision: Explaining the Cuban Missile Crisis* (Boston: Little, Brown, 1971); and Scott A. Snook, *Friendly Fire: The Accidental Shootdown of U.S. Black Hawks over Northern Iraq* (Princeton, NJ: Princeton University Press, 2000).

16. Matthai Kurvila, "In Islamic Crisis, Islamic Funds Profit on Faith," *San Francisco Chronicle*, February 9, 2009.

17. Ian I. Mitroff, *Why Some Companies Emerge Stronger and Better from a Crisis* (New York: Amacom, 2005); Ian I. Mitroff, *Crisis Leadership: Planning for the Unthinkable* (New York: John Wiley, 2003); and Ian I. Mitroff and Gus Anagnos, *Managing Crises Before They Happen* (New York: Amacom, 2000).

18. For academic research that focuses on a broad range of variables, see Snook, *Friendly Fire*; and Roberto, "Lessons From Everest."

CHAPTER I

1. Ian I. Mitroff, Can M. Alpaslan, and Sandy E. Green, "Crises as Ill-Structured Messes: Philosophical Issues of Crisis Management," *International Studies Review* 6, no. 1 (2004): 175–82.

2. For a more academic and comprehensive definition, see Chris M.

Pearson and Judith A. Clair, "Reframing Crisis Management," *Academy of Management Review* 23, no. 1 (1998): 59–77.

3. Thierry C. Pauchant and Ian I. Mitroff, *Transforming the Crisis-Prone Organization: Preventing Individual, Organizational, and Environmental Tragedies* (San Francisco: Jossey-Bass, 1993); Karl E. Weick, "The Collapse of Sensemaking in Organizations: The Mann Gulch Disaster," *Administrative Science Quarterly* 38 (1993): 628–52; and Ronnie Janoff-Bulman, *Shattered Assumptions. Towards a New Psychology of Trauma* (New York: New Press, 1992).

4. What is especially disconcerting is that, with surprisingly little modification, many of the same kinds of assumptions apply to the current financial crisis. To be sure, we would have to change some of the basic terms, such as *terrorist*, but even this is debatable. It is not an exaggeration in the slightest to say that those to whom we entrusted our financial futures, Bernie Madoff for example, behaved like "terrorists" with regard to our financial well-being. They certainly did as much damage to the worldwide financial system as any group of terrorists could have done. And of course, we would have to add other assumptions such as "Housing prices will always continue to rise," "We can trust those on Wall Street to act not solely in their interests alone," "Those in charge actually understand and know what they are doing with the complex financial instruments they invented," "The government will protect us," "The markets are rational and efficient," and so on.

5. Lisa A. Mainiero and Donald E. Gibson, "Managing Employee Trauma: Dealing with the Emotional Fallout from 9-11," *Academy of Management Executive* 17, no. 3 (2003): 130.

6. Godfrey Hodgson, *The Myth of American Exceptionalism* (New Haven, CT: Yale University Press, 2009).

7. George Akerlof and Robert Shiller, *Animal Spirits: How Human Psychology Drives the Economy and Why It Matters for Global Capitalism* (Princeton, NJ: Princeton University Press, 2009).

8. Jocelyn Pixley, *Emotions in Finance* (Cambridge, UK: Cambridge University Press, 2004).

9. Oliver E. Williamson, *The Economic Institutions of Capitalism: Firms, Markets, Relational Contracting* (New York: Free Press, 1985); and Michael C. Jensen and William H. Meckling, "Theory of the Firm: Managerial Behavior, Agency Costs and Ownership Structure," *Journal of Financial Economics* 3 (1976): 305–60.

10. See also Kathleen J. Tierney, "From the Margins to the Main-stream? Disaster Research at the Crossroads," *Annual Review of Sociology* 33 (2007): 503–25.

11. See Carl G. Jung, *The Collected Works of Carl Jung, Volume 6: Psychological Types*, edited and translated by Gerhard Adler and R.F.C. Hull (Princeton, NJ: Princeton University Press, 1971); Isabel Briggs Myers, *Gifts Differing* (Palo Alto, CA: Consulting Psychologists Press, 1980). See also Ian I. Mitroff, *Crisis Leadership: Planning for the Unthinkable* (New York: John Wiley, 2003).

12. The strength of the Myers-Briggs framework for us is its versatile conceptual framework. Specifically, it is one of the very few frameworks that can represent simultaneously and parsimoniously the very fundamental dichotomies of parts versus wholes, things versus people, details versus big picture, technical versus social, thinking versus feeling, particular versus universal, one versus many, and present versus future.

CHAPTER 2

1. Russell L. Ackoff, *Re-Creating the Corporation* (New York: Oxford University Press, 1999), 324.

2. Ibid., 178–79.

3. Parts of this discussion are taken from Ian I. Mitroff and Abraham Silvers, *Dirty Rotten Strategies: How We Trick Ourselves and Others into Solving the Wrong Problems Precisely* (Palo Alto, CA: Stanford University Press, 2009).

4. Horst Rittel and Melvin Webber, "Dilemmas in a General Theory of Planning," *Policy Sciences* 4 (1973): 155–69.

5. U.S. Department of Labor, Bureau of Labor Statistics, "Labor Force Statistics from the Current Population," http://www.bls.gov/cps (accessed December 17, 2010).

6. We will attempt to explain this "mess" and its broader contexts in Chapter 8.

7. Bob Herbert, "A World of Hurt," *New York Times*, September 15, 2009.

8. Karen Ho, *Liquidated: An Ethnography of Wall Street* (Durham, NC: Duke University Press, 2009).

9. Ibid.

10. Kevin Phillips, *Bad Money* (New York: Viking, 2008).

11. Barbara Ehrenreich and Dedrick Muhammad, "The Recession's Racial Divide," *New York Times*, Sunday Opinion, September 13, 2009.

CHAPTER 3

1. Steven Spear, "Fixing Health Care from the Inside, Today," *Harvard Business Review* (September 2005).

2. Regina E. Herzlinger, "Why Innovation in Health Care Is So Hard," *Harvard Business Review* (May 2006).

3. Sam Mirmirani, "The United States Health Care System in Crisis: Its Origins and Future Outlook," *Business Review* 13, no. 1 (2009): 74–79. See also Paul Fronstin, "Sources of Health Insurance and Characteristics of the Uninsured: Analysis of the March 2009 Current Population Survey," *Employee Benefit Research Institute*, no. 334 (September 2009).

4. Richard Hofstader, *The Paranoid Style of American Politics* (Cambridge, MA: Harvard University Press, 1952).

5. Allen C. Amason, "Distinguishing the Effects of Functional and Dysfunctional Conflict on Strategic Decision Making: Resolving a Paradox for Top Management Teams," *Academy of Management Journal* 39, no. 1 (1996): 123–48; and Ian I. Mitroff, "Dialectic Squared: A Fundamental Difference in Perception on the Meanings of Some Key Concepts in Social Science," *Decision Sciences* 13 (1982): 222–24.

6. Amason, "Distinguishing the Effects of Functional and Dysfunctional Conflict on Strategic Decision Making."

7. Michael Roberto, *Managing for Conflict and Consensus: Why Great Leaders Don't Take Yes for an Answer* (Philadelphia: Wharton School Publishing, 2005).

8. Ian I. Mitroff and Gus Anagnos, *Managing Crises Before They Happen* (New York: Amacom, 2000); and Stephan Gundel, "Towards a New Typology of Crises," *Journal of Contingencies and Crisis Management* 13, no. 3 (2005): 106–15.

9. Ian I. Mitroff, *Why Some Companies Emerge Stronger and Better from a Crisis* (New York: Amacom, 2005); Ian I. Mitroff, *Crisis Leadership: Planning for the Unthinkable* (New York: John Wiley, 2003); Mitroff and Anagnos, *Managing Crises Before They Happen*; and Thierry Pauchant and Ian I. Mitroff, *Transforming the Crisis Prone Organization* (San Francisco: Jossey-Bass, 1992).

10. Scholars have developed several crisis typologies. See Alfred Marcus

and Robert Goodman, "Victims and Shareholders: The Dilemma of Presenting Corporate Policy During a Crisis," *Academy of Management Journal* 34, no. 2 (1991): 281–305; Ian I. Mitroff and Can M. Alpaslan, "Preparing for Evil," *Harvard Business Review* 81, no. 4 (2003): 109–15; and Gundel, "Towards a New Typology of Crises.

11. Hofstader, *The Paranoid Style of American Politics.*

12. Stephen H. Long, M. Susan Marquis, and Jack Rodgers, "Do People Shift Their Use of Health Services Over Time to Take Advantage of Insurance?" *Journal of Health Economics* 17, no. 1 (1998): 105–15.

13. The authors wish to thank Emery Roe for these suggestions.

CHAPTER 4

1. Peter Salovey and John D. Mayer, "Emotional Intelligence," *Imagination, Cognition, and Personality* (1990): 9, 185–211; Daniel Goleman, *Emotional Intelligence* (New York: Bantam Books, 1995); and John D. Mayer, Peter Salovey, and David R. Caruso, "Emotional Intelligence: Theory, Findings, and Implications," *Psychological Inquiry* 60 (2004): 197–215.

2. Louis Sahagun, "Boy's Bear Hunt Wish Puts Foundation in Cross Hairs, Animal Activists Up in Arms at Make-A-Wish for Allowing Dying Teenager to Kill a Kodiac in Alaska," *Los Angeles Times*, May 11, 1996.

3. Ibid.

4. Lawrence Kohlberg, *Essays on Moral Development* (San Francisco: Harper & Row, 1981); James R. Rest, *Moral Development: Advances in Research and Theory* (New York: Praeger, 1986).

5. Johann Hari, "The Wrong Kind of Green: How Conservation Groups Are Bargaining Away Our Future," *Nation*, March 22, 2010.

6. Diane Vaughan, *The Challenger Launch Decision: Risky Technology, Culture and Deviance at NASA* (Chicago and London: University of Chicago Press, 1996); Diane Vaughan, "NASA Revisited: Theory, Analogy, and Public Sociology," *American Journal of Sociology* 112, no. 2 (2006): 353–93.

7. Ibid.

8. Kendra Marr, "Toyota Passes General Motors as World's Largest Carmaker," *Washington Post*, January 22, 2009, http://www.washington post.com/wp-dyn/content/article/2009/01/21/AR2009012101216.html (accessed August 3, 2010).

9. Milton Friedman, "The Social Responsibility of Business Is to In-

crease Profits," *New York Times Magazine* 13 (1970): 32; Michael C. Jensen and William H. Meckling, "Theory of the Firm: Managerial Behavior, Agency Costs and Ownership Structure," *Journal of Financial Economics* 3 (1976): 305–60.

10. Margaret M. Blair, *Ownership and Control: Rethinking Corporate Governance for the Twenty-First Century* (Washington, DC: The Brookings Institution, 1995); and Frank Easterbrook and Daniel R. Fischel, *The Economic Structure of Corporate Law* (Cambridge, MA: Harvard University Press, 1991).

11. Note that a shareholder is a stakeholder. *Stakeholder* is a broad term and includes an organization's shareholders as well as its suppliers, creditors, employees, communities, customers, and so on.

12. Can M. Alpaslan, Sandy E. Green, and Ian I. Mitroff, "Corporate Governance in the Context of Crises: Towards a Stakeholder Theory of Crisis Management," *Journal of Contingencies and Crisis Management* 17, no. 1 (2009): 38–49.

13. William D. Ross, *The Right and the Good* (Oxford, UK: Clarendon Press, 1930).

14. Can M. Alpaslan, "Ethical Management of Crises: Shareholder Value Maximization or Stakeholder Loss Minimization?" *Journal of Corporate Citizenship* 36 (2009): 41–50.

15. Jonathan Haidt, "The Moral Emotions," in Richard J. Davidson, Klaus R. Scherer, and H. Hill Goldsmith (eds.), *Handbook of Affective Sciences* (Oxford: Oxford University Press, 2003): 852–70.

CHAPTER 5

1. For an in-depth treatment of many of these same assumptions that constitute the culture of Wall Street, see Karen Ho, *Liquidated: An Ethnography of Wall Street* (Durham, NC: Duke University Press, 2009).

2. See, for example, Sim B. Sitkin and Amy L. Pablo, "Reconceptualizing the Determinants of Risk Behavior," *Academy of Management Review* 17 (1992): 21–22.

3. Ibid.

4. For a similar point made by a behavioral economist, see Hersh Shefrin, *Ending the Management Illusion: How to Drive Business Results Using the Principles of Behavioral Finance* (Columbus, OH: McGraw-Hill, 2008).

5. Charles P. Kindleberger, *Manias, Panics, and Crashes: A History of Financial Crises*, 4th ed. (New York: John Wiley, 2000).

6. Although they are not uncommon. See Ho, *Liquidated*.

7. Ian I. Mitroff, *Stakeholders of the Organizational Mind: Toward a New View of Organizational Policy Making* (San Francisco: Jossey-Bass, 1983); and Edgar Schein, *Organizational Culture and Leadership: A Dynamic View* (San Francisco: Jossey-Bass, 1985).

8. To see how the characteristics of an industry influence company culture and behavior, see George G. Gordon, "Industry Determinants of Organizational Culture," *Academy of Management Review* 16, no. 2 (1991): 396.

9. Ho, *Liquidated*.

10. Bethany McLean and Peter Elkind, *Smartest Guys in the Room: The Amazing Rise and Scandalous Fall of Enron* (New York: Penguin Group, 2003).

11. Interested readers may read Joel Bakan's *The Corporation: The Pathological Pursuit of Profit and Power* (Columbus, OH: Free Press, 2004) to see a similar argument. In the book, the author makes the case that if corporations had a personality, it would be one of a psychopath.

12. American Psychiatric Association, *Diagnostic and Statistical Manual of Mental Disorders*, 4th ed., Text Revision (Washington, DC: American Psychiatric Association, 2000): 717. See also Tim Hall, "New Narc City: Sam Vaknin and the Narcissism of Wall Street," *New York Press*, February 18, 2003, http://www.nypress.com/article-7043-new-narc-city -sam-vaknin-and-the-narcissism-of-wall-street.html (accessed August 3, 2010); and Kevin A. Hassett, "Harvard Narcissists with MBAs Killed Wall Street," *Bloomberg*, February 17, 2009, http://www.bloomberg.com/apps /news?pid=newsarchive&sid=a_ac69DqFutQ (accessed August 3, 2010).

13. Anna Freud, *The Ego and the Mechanisms of Defense* (New York: International Universities Press, 1967).

14. Carl Jung, *The Archetypes and the Collective Unconscious*, 2nd ed. (Princeton, NJ: Bollingen, 1968), 284.

15. Martin L. Bowles, "The Organization Shadow," *Organization Studies* 12, no. 3 (1991): 387.

16. Ken Wilber, *Collected Works of Ken Wilber*, vol. 2 (Boston: Shambhala, 1999): 600–601.

17. Hyman Minsky, "The Financial Instability Hypothesis," working paper #74, the Jerome Levy Economics Institute of Bard College, 1992, 7–8.

18. Thierry C. Pauchant and Ian I. Mitroff, *Transforming the Crisis-Prone Organization: Preventing Individual, Organizational, and Environmental Tragedies* (San Francisco: Jossey-Bass, 1992); and Christine M. Pearson and Ian I. Mitroff, "From Crisis-Prone to Crisis-Prepared," *Academy of Management Executive* 7, no. 1 (1993): 48–59.

19. Ibid.

20. Ian I. Mitroff and Thierry C. Pauchant, *We're So Big and Powerful Nothing Bad Can Happen to Us: An Investigation of America's Crisis Prone Corporations* (Secaucus, NJ: Carol Publishing Group, 1990).

CHAPTER 6

1. Christine M. Pearson and Judith A. Clair, "Reframing Crisis Management," *Academy of Management Review* 23, no. 1 (1998): 59–77; Ronnie Janoff-Bulman, *Shattered Assumptions: Towards a New Psychology of Trauma* (New York: New Press, 1992); and Shelley Taylor, "Adjustment to Threatening Events," *American Psychologist* 38 (1983): 1161–73.

2. Ian I. Mitroff and Thierry C. Pauchant, *We're So Big and Powerful Nothing Bad Can Happen to Us: An Investigation of America's Crisis Prone Corporations* (Secaucus, NJ: Carol Publishing Group, 1990).

3. Barry M. Staw, Lance E. Sandelands, and Jane E. Dutton, "Threat-Rigidity Effects in Organizational Behavior: A Multilevel Analysis," *Administrative Science Quarterly* 26, no. 4 (1981): 501–24.

4. Ibid.

5. Christine M. Pearson and Ian I. Mitroff, "From Crisis-Prone to Crisis-Prepared," *Academy of Management Executive* 7, no. 1 (1993): 48–59; and Pearson and Clair, "Reframing Crisis Management."

6. Les Coleman, "Frequency of Man-Made Disasters in the 20th Century," *Journal of Contingencies and Crisis Management* 14, no. 1 (2006): 3–11.

7. Ian I. Mitroff, Paul Shrivastava, and Firdaus E. Udwadia, "Effective Crisis Management," *Academy of Management Executive* 1, no. 4 (1987): 283–92.

8. Ibid.

9. Ibid.

10. Cathy B. Thomas, "Called to Account," *Time*, June 18, 2002.

11. Joseph L. Bower and Stuart C. Gilson, "The Social Cost of Fraud and Bankruptcy," *Harvard Business Review* (December 2003): 1–3.

12. Institute of the Analysis of Global Security, "How Much Did the September 11 Terrorist Attack Cost America?" http://www.iags.org/costof911.html (accessed Oct. 16, 2009).

13. International Monetary Fund, "Global Financial Stability Report: Navigating the Financial Challenges Ahead," October 2009, http://www.imf.org/external/pubs/ft/gfsr/2009/02/index.htm (accessed August 3, 2010).

14. Les Coleman, "The Frequency and Cost of Corporate Crises 1," *Journal of Contingencies and Crisis Management* 12, no. 1 (2004): 2.

15. Can M. Alpaslan, "Corporate Ethical Orientation and Crisis Management, Before and After 9/11," PhD dissertation under supervision of Ian Mitroff, University of Southern California, 2004.

16. Rodney C. Runyan, "Small Business in the Face of Crisis: Identifying Barriers to Recovery from a Natural Disaster," *Journal of Contingencies and Crisis Management* 14, no. 1 (2006): 12–26; Les Coleman and Ira Helsloot, "On the Need for Quantifying Corporate Crises and Other Man-Made Disasters," *Journal of Contingencies and Crisis Management* 15, no. 3 (2007); Ian I. Mitroff and Can M. Alpaslan, "Preparing for Evil," *Harvard Business Review* 81, no. 4 (2003): 109–15; Pearson and Mitroff, "From Crisis-Prone to Crisis-Prepared"; Zachary Sheaffer and Rita Mano-Negrin, "Executives' Orientations as Indicators of Crisis Management Policies and Practices," *Journal of Management Studies* 40, no. 2 (2003): 573–606; and Sandra Waddock and Neil Smith, "Corporate Responsibility Audits: Doing Well by Doing Good," *Sloan Management Review* 41, no. 2 (2000): 75–83.

17. Pearson and Mitroff, "From Crisis-Prone to Crisis-Prepared"; Mitroff and Alpaslan, "Preparing for Evil"; and Alpaslan, "Corporate Ethical Orientation and Crisis Management." Note also that there aren't many theoretical and empirical studies that focus on the mechanisms by which successful crisis management behavior and outcomes affect the bottom line.

18. John F. Preble, "Integrating the Crisis Management Perspective into the Strategic Management Process," *Journal of Management Studies* 34, no. 5 (1997): 769–91.

19. Ian I. Mitroff, Christine M. Pearson, and L. Katharine Harrington, *The Essential Guide to Managing Corporate Crises* (New York: Oxford University Press, 1996); Paul Shrivastava, Ian I. Mitroff, Danny Miller,

and Anil Miglani, "Understanding Organizational Crises," *Journal of Management Studies* 25, no. 4 (1988): 285–303; Thierry C. Pauchant and Ian I. Mitroff, *Transforming the Crisis-Prone Organization: Preventing Individual, Organizational, and Environmental Tragedies* (San Francisco: Jossey-Bass, 1992); and Karl E. Weick, "Enacted Sensemaking in Crisis Situations," *Journal of Management Studies* 25, no. 4 (1988): 305–17.

20. Can M. Alpaslan, Sandy E. Green, and Ian I. Mitroff, "Corporate Governance in the Context of Crises: Towards a Stakeholder Theory of Crisis Management," *Journal of Contingencies and Crisis Management* 17, no. 1 (2009): 38; Les Coleman, "Frequency of Man-Made Disasters in the 20th Century," *Journal of Contingencies and Crisis Management* 14, no. 1 (2006): 3–11; and Can M. Alpaslan, "Ethical Management of Crises," *Journal of Corporate Citizenship* (2009): 41–50.

21. Uriel Rosenthal, Arjen Boin, and Luise Comfort, *Managing Crises: Threats, Dilemmas, Opportunities* (Springfield, IL: Charles Thomas, 2001); Patric Lagadec, "Learning Processes for Crisis Management in Complex Organizations," *Journal of Contingencies and Crisis Management* 5, no. 1 (1997): 24–31; Jack V. Michaels, *Technical Risk Management* (Upper Saddle River, NJ: Prentice-Hall, 1996); Ian I. Mitroff, *Why Some Companies Emerge Stronger and Better from a Crisis: Seven Essential Lessons for Surviving Disaster* (New York: Amacom, 2005); Ian I. Mitroff and Gus Anagnos, *Managing Crises Before They Happen: What Every Executive and Manager Needs to Know About Crisis Management* (New York: Amacom, 2001); Arjen Boin and Paul Hart "Public Leadership in Times of Crisis: Mission Impossible?" *Public Administration Review* 63, no. 5 (2003): 544; Peter Schwartz, *Inevitable Surprises: Thinking Ahead in Times of Turbulence* (New York: Gotham, 2003); and Karl E. Weick and Kathleen M. Sutcliffe, *Managing the Unexpected: Assuring High Performance in an Age of Complexity* (San Francisco: Jossey-Bass, 2003).

22. See, for example, Manfred F. R. Kets de Vries and Danny Miller, *The Neurotic Organization: Diagnosing and Changing Counterproductive Styles of Management* (San Francisco: Jossey-Bass, 1984); see also Manfred F. R. Kets de Vries, "Organizations on the Couch: A Clinical Perspective on Organizational Dynamics," *European Management Journal* 22, no. 2 (2004): 183–200.

23. Roger D. Evered and James C. Selman, "Coaching and the Art of Management," *Organizational Dynamics* (Winter 1989): 16–32; Richard R.

Kilburg (ed.), "Executive Coaching," special issue, *Consulting Psychology Journal: Practice and Research* 48, no. 2 (1996); Lee Smith, "The Executive's New Coach," *Fortune*, December 27, 1993; and Bertram C. Edelstein and David J. Armstrong, "A Model for Executive Development," *Human Resource Planning* 16, no. 4 (1993): 46–51.

24. Vicki Hart, John Blattner, and Staci Leipsic, "Coaching Versus Therapy: A Perspective," *Consulting Psychology Journal: Practice and Research* 53, no. 4 (2001): 229–37.

25. Douglas T. Hall, Karen L. Otazo, and George I. Hollenbeck, "Behind Closed Doors: What Really Happens in Executive Coaching," *Organizational Dynamics* (Winter 1999): 39–53.

26. Richard R. Kilburg, *Executive Coaching: Developing Managerial Wisdom in a World of Chaos* (Washington, DC: American Psychological Association, 2000).

27. John Bowlby, *A Secure Base: Parent-Child Attachment and Healthy Human Development* (New York: Basic Books, 1988); William A. Kahn and Kathy E. Kram, "Authority at Work: Internal Models and Their Organizational Consequences," *Academy of Management Review* 19, no. 1 (1994): 17–50; Mario Mikulincer and Victor Florian, "Appraisal of and Coping with a Real-Life Stressful Situation: The Contribution of Attachment Styles," *Personality and Social Psychology Bulletin* 21, no. 4 (1995): 406–14; Mario Mikulincer and Victor Florian, *The Relationship Between Adult Attachment Styles and Emotional and Cognitive Reactions to Stressful Events*, in J. A. Simpson and W. S. Rholes (eds.), *Attachment Theory and Close Relationships* (New York: Guilford Press, 1998), 143–65; Mario Mikulincer, Victor Florian, and Aron Weller, "Attachment Styles, Coping Strategies, and Posttraumatic Psychological Distress: The Impact of the Gulf War in Israel," *Journal of Personality and Social Psychology* 64, no. 5 (1993): 817–26; and Olya Khaleelee, "The Use of the Defense Mechanism Test to Aid in Understanding the Personality of Senior Executives and the Implications for Their Careers," *Rorschachiana* 30 (2009): 73–96.

28. Carl Rogers, *On Becoming a Person: A Therapist's View of Psychotherapy* (London: Constable, 1961); and Carl Rogers, *A Way of Being* (Boston: Houghton-Mifflin, 1989).

29. Manfred F. R. Kets de Vries, *The Leader on the Couch: A Clinical Approach to Changing People and Organizations* (San Francisco: Jossey-Bass, 2006).

30. Manfred F. R. Kets de Vries and Konstantin Korotov, "Creating Transformational Executive Education Programs," *Academy of Management Learning & Education* 6, no. 3 (2007): 375–87.

31. John F. McCarthy, David J. O'Connell, and Douglas T. Hall, "Leading Beyond Tragedy: The Balance of Personal Identity and Adaptability," *Leadership & Organization Development Journal* 26, no. 5/6 (2005): 458.

32. Kets de Vries and Miller, *The Neurotic Organization*. See also Kets de Vries, *The Leader on the Couch*.

33. Andrew D. Brown and Ken Starkey, "Organizational Identity and Learning: A Psychodynamic Perspective," *Academy of Management Review* 25, no. 1 (2000): 102–20. See also Andrew D. Brown, "Narcissism, Identity, and Legitimacy," *Academy of Management Review* 22, no. 3 (1997): 643.

34. Melanie Klein, *Contributions to Psychoanalysis* (London: Hogarth, 1948).

35. For an example of splitting, see Mitroff and Anagnos, *Managing Crises Before They Happen*. On pages 90–92, the authors discuss how the top management of ValuJet, an airliner that declared bankruptcy after one of its aircraft crashed in the Florida Everglades, engaged in vigorous denial, blamed the media for vilifying ValuJet, and proclaimed that they were the real victims.

36. Abraham Maslow, "A Theory of Human Motivation," *Psychology Review* 50 (1943): 370–96; David R. Hawkins, *Power vs. Force: The Hidden Determinants of Human Behavior* (New York: Hay House, 2002), 68–69; Lawrence Kohlberg, *Essays on Moral Development, Vol. I: The Philosophy of Moral Development* (San Francisco: Harper & Row, 1981); Carol Gilligan, *In a Different Voice* (Cambridge, MA: Harvard University Press, 1982); and George E. Vaillant, *Adaptation to Life* (Boston: Little, Brown, 1977). For a much broader set of developmental lines, see Ken Wilber, *Integral Psychology* (Boston: Shambhala, 2000).

37. Hawkins, *Power vs. Force*, 240–42.

38. Ibid., 242–43.

39. George Vaillant, Michael Bond, and Caroline Vaillant, "An Empirically Validated Hierarchy of Defense Mechanisms," *Archives of General Psychiatry* 43 (1986): 786–94. See also Glen O. Gabbard, *Psychodynamic Psychiatry in Clinical Practice*, 3rd ed. (Washington, DC: American Psychiatric Press, 2000).

40. See Ibid. See also Ian I. Mitroff and Thierry C. Pauchant, *The*

Environmental & Business Disasters Book: How Big Business Avoids Responsibility for Its Catastrophes (New York: Shapolsky, 1990).

41. Alpaslan, Green, and Mitroff, "Corporate Governance in the Context of Crises." Also see Vaillant, Bond, and Valliant, "An Empirically Validated Hierarchy of Defense Mechanisms."

42. For a moral development framework, see Kohlberg, *Essays on Moral Development, Vol. I*; and Gilligan, *In a Different Voice*. For a cognitive development framework, see Jean Piaget, *The Essential Piaget*, ed. Howard E. Gruber and J. Jacques Voneche (New York: Basic Books, 1977). For a psychosocial development framework, see Erik H. Erikson, *Identity and the Life Cycle* (New York: International Universities Press, 1959). For a developmental framework that focuses on general values, see Don E. Beck and Christopher Cowan, *Spiral Dynamics: Mastering Values, Leadership, and Change* (Malden, MA: Blackwell, 1996).

43. For a comprehensive overview of developmental frameworks, see Wilber, *Integral Psychology*. See also the works cited above.

CHAPTER 7

1. Figure 7.1 is a modified version of the Diamond Model of Crisis Management presented in Ian I. Mitroff, Can M. Alpaslan, and Sandy E. Green, "Crises as Ill-Structured Messes: Philosophical Issues of Crisis Management," *International Studies Review* 6, no. 1 (2004): 175–82. Also see Ian I. Mitroff and Francisco Sagasti, "Epistemology as General Systems Theory: An Approach to the Design of Complex Decision-Making Experiments," *Philosophy of the Social Sciences* 3 (1973): 117–34.

2. The point of Figure 7.1 is not to confuse the reader but to say that all of the programs shown in Figure 7.1 are required in order to manage crises successfully. No one believes that a business strategy can be successful without its managers having a fundamental understanding of marketing, management, finance, accounting, economics, operations, and human resources activities that must be performed every day. Similarly, for a business to survive a crisis, managers need to have a basic understanding of all the programs shown in Figure 7.1.

3. For an academic and comprehensive review of crisis communications, see W. Timothy Coombs, *Ongoing Crisis Communication: Planning, Managing, and Responding*, 2nd ed. (Thousand Oaks, CA: Sage, 2007).

4. For a comprehensive review of emergency management (mitigation,

response, and recovery), see George Haddow, Jane Bullock, and Damon P. Coppola, *Introduction to Emergency Management*, 3rd ed., Homeland Security Series (n.p.: Butterworth-Heinemann, 2007).

5. Charles Perrow, "Organizing to Reduce the Vulnerabilities of Complexity," *Journal of Contingencies and Crisis Management* 7, no. 3 (1999): 150–55; and Karlene H. Roberts, "Some Characteristics of One Type of High-Reliability Organization," *Organization Science* 1 (1990): 60–176.

6. There are of course many more than just five ways of producing knowledge, or more generally, systems of inquiry. The contention that there are just five systems and five alone is absurd. Indeed, what form of inquiry would we have to use to determine that there are five and only five such systems? The five that are covered in this chapter are merely a good starting point. For a more in-depth treatment of the five systems, see C. West Churchman, *The Design of Inquiring Systems* (New York: Basic Books, 1971); Edgar A. Singer Jr., *Experience and Reflection* (Philadelphia: University of Pennsylvania Press, 1959); and Ian I. Mitroff and Harold A. Linstone, *The Unbounded Mind: Breaking the Chains of Traditional Thinking* (New York: Oxford University Press, 1993).

7. This example is taken from several student papers from Ian I. Mitroff's classes.

8. An inquiry system consists of inputs and an operator that transforms the inputs into outputs, which are then regarded as the "truth." One of the most critical features of an inquiry system is what Churchman labels the "guarantor." The guarantor is that feature of an inquiry system that "guarantees" that if one starts with the "right kind of inputs" and operates on them in the "right way," then the output(s) of the system will be the "truth." In the first model, the tighter the agreement among experts, that is, the stronger the agreement among them, supposedly the "more" the agreement is or approaches the truth. Thus, in the first model, the guarantor is the agreement among independent experts. Notice that the guarantor and the operator are confounded. That is, they are not independent. Agreement is the operator—it is used to manufacture or to produce the output—and agreement is also the guarantor of the system as well. For this reason, one is well advised to be suspicious of how agreement is obtained, for example, whether it is forced or not.

9. Michael Kinsley, "In Defense of Partisan Bickering," *Time*, February 5, 2007.

10. There is nothing wrong per se in using one method initially to select another method of reaching an important decision. Once we have all of the various methods at our disposal, we can use them in various combinations. The important point is that pure methods, systems, or models themselves are rarely discussed in the arena of business, let alone their combinations.

11. See note 10.

12. Quoted in David Marcum and Steven Smith, *Egonomics* (New York: Simon & Schuster, 2007), 132.

13. Churchman, *The Design of Inquiring Systems*; and Singer, *Experience and Reflection*.

14. Russell L. Ackoff and C. West Churchman, *Methods of Inquiry: An Introduction to Philosophy and Scientific Method* (St. Louis: Educational Publishers, 1950).

15. Ian I. Mitroff, *The Subjective Side of Science: A Philosophical Inquiry into the Psychology of the Apollo Moon Scientists* (Amsterdam, The Netherlands: Elsevier, 1974).

16. John Dewey, *The Quest for Certainty* (New York: Putnam, 1960).

17. E. J. Dionne Jr., "The Meaning of Bipartisanship Talk—Nothing," *San Francisco Chronicle*, January 9, 2007.

CHAPTER 8

1. Ian I. Mitroff, *The Subjective Side of Science* (Amsterdam, The Netherlands: Elsevier, 1974).

2. Mark Granovetter, "Economic Action and Social Structure: the Problem of Embeddedness," *American Journal of Sociology* 91 (1985): 481–510.

3. For a recent review of the field, see Linton Freeman, *The Development of Social Network Analysis* (Vancouver, Canada: Empirical Press, 2006).

4. For instance, in Chapter 7, the different consciousness levels we have mentioned are based on human development studies. In Chapter 6, some of the strategies to overcome denial are based on studies conducted in the fields of psychology and psychoanalysis.

5. An excellent example of perspective 4 is Karen Ho's ethnographic study of Wall Street, which we have cited heavily in Chapter 5.

6. For a more comprehensive set of perspectives on risk, see Catherine E. Althaus, "A Disciplinary Perspective on the Epistemological Status of Risk," *Risk Analysis* 25, no. 3 (2005).

7. Deborah Lupton, *Risk* (London: Routledge, 1999); and Robert P.

Gephart Jr., John Van Maanen, and Thomas Oberlechner, "Organizations and Risk in Late Modernity," *Organization Studies* 30 (2009): 141.

8. Harry M. Markowitz, "Portfolio Selection," *Journal of Finance* 7, no. 1 (1952): 77–91.

9. James Burke, *Chances: The Probability Factors of Life* (London: Virgin Books, 1991).

10. Charles Perrow, *Normal Accidents: Living with High-Risk Technologies* (Basic Books: New York, 1984); and Charles Perrow, *Complex Organizations: A Critical Essay* (New York: McGraw-Hill, 1993).

11. Ulrich Beck, *Risk Society: Towards a New Modernity* (London: Sage, 1992); and Anthony Giddens, "Risk and Responsibility," *Modern Law Journal* 62, no. 1 (1991): 4.

12. Daniel Kahneman and Amos Tversky, "Prospect Theory: An Analysis of Decision Under Risk," *Econometrica* 48 (1979): 263–91; Baruch Fischhoff and others, *Acceptable Risk* (Cambridge, UK: Cambridge University Press, 1981); and Paul Slovic, *The Perception of Risk* (London: Earthscan Publications, 2000).

13. Mary Douglas, *Risk and Blame: Essays in Cultural Theory* (London: Routledge, 1992); Mary Douglas and Aaron Wildavsky, *Risk and Culture: An Essay on the Selection of Technical and Environmental Dangers* (Berkeley: University of California Press, 1982).

14. Karl E. Weick, "The Collapse of Sensemaking in Organizations: The Mann Gulch Disaster," *Administrative Science Quarterly* 38, no. 4 (1993): 628–52.

15. Richard Thaler, "From Homo Economicus to Homo Sapiens," *Journal of Economic Perspectives* 14, no. 1 (2000): 133–41.

16. Jocelyn Pixley, *Emotions in Finance* (Cambridge, UK: Cambridge University Press, 2004).

17. Jane J. Mansbridge (ed.), *Beyond Self-Interest* (Chicago: University of Chicago Press, 1990).

18. Justin Fox, *The Myth of the Rational Market* (n.p.: HarperBusiness, 2009).

19. Ibid.

20. Harry Markowitz, "Portfolio Selection," *Journal of Finance* 7, no. 1 (1952): 77–91.

21. Ibid.

22. Ibid.

23. Milton Friedman, "The Methodology of Positive Economics," in *Essays in Positive Economics* (Chicago: University of Chicago Press, 1953), 3–43.

24. Ibid.

25. Robert H. Frank, Thomas Gilovich, and Dennis T. Regan, "Does Studying Economics Inhibit Cooperation?" *Journal of Economic Perspectives* 7, no. 2 (1993): 159–71; Fabrizio Ferraro, Jeffrey Pfeffer, and Robert I. Sutton, "Economics Language and Assumptions: How Theories Can Become Self-Fulfilling," *Academy of Management Review* 30, no. 1 (2005): 8–24.

26. Donald Mackenzie, "Long-Term Capital Management and the Sociology of Arbitrage," *Economy and Society* 32, no. 3 (2003): 349–80.

27. Roger Lowenstein, *When Genius Failed: The Rise and Fall of Long-Term Capital Management* (New York: Random House, 2000).

28. Felix Salmon, "Recipe for Disaster: The Formula That Killed Wall Street," *Wired Magazine*, Feb. 23, 2009.

29. Morningstar "Goldman Sachs Group Inc," key ratios report, http://financials.morningstar.com/ratios/r.html?t=GS (accessed August 3, 2010); Morningstar "Morgan Stanley," key ratios report, http://financials.morningstar.com/ratios/r.html?t=MS (accessed August 3, 2010); Morningstar "Apple Inc," key ratios report, http://financials.morningstar.com/ratios/r.html?t=AAPL (accessed August 3, 2010); and Morningstar "Johnson & Johnson," key ratios report, http://financials.morningstar.com/ratios/r.html?t=JNJ (accessed August 3, 2010).

30. Ibid.

31. Gerald Davis, "The Rise and Fall of Finance and the End of the Society of Organizations," *Academy of Management Perspectives* 23, no. 3 (2009): 27–44.

32. Ibid.

33. Adolf A. Berle Jr. and Gardiner Means, *The Modern Corporation and Private Property* (New York: Macmillan, 1932).

34. Michael C. Jensen, "Value Maximization, Stakeholder Theory, and the Corporate Objective Function," *Business Ethics Quarterly* 12, no. 2 (2002): 235–56; and Anant K. Sundaram and Andrew C. Inkpen, "The Corporate Objective Revisited," *Organization Science* 15, no. 3 (2004): 350–63.

35. Alan Greenspan and James Kennedy, "Sources and Uses of Equity

Extracted from Homes," *Oxford Review of Economic Policy* 24, no. 1 (2008): 120–44.

36. Davis, "The Rise and Fall of Finance," 28, 44.

37. Ibid.

38. Daniel Yergin, *The Commanding Heights: The Battle for the World Economy* (New York: Free Press, 2002).

39. Charles P. Kindleberger, *Manias, Panics, and Crashes: A History of Financial Crises,* 4th ed. (New York: John Wiley, 2000).

40. Ibid.

41. Robert Shiller, *The Subprime Solution* (Princeton, NJ: Princeton University Press, 2008).

42. George Akerlof and Robert Shiller, *Animal Spirits: How Human Psychology Drives the Economy and Why It Matters for Global Capitalism* (Princeton, NJ: Princeton University Press, 2009).

43. Aristotle, *The Art of Rhetoric*, ed. Hugh Lawson-Tancred (New York: Penguin Books, 1991); Patricia Bizzell and Bruce Herzberg (eds.), *The Rhetorical Tradition: Readings from Classical Times to the Present* (Boston: Bedford Books of St. Martin's Press, 1990); Sandy E. Green Jr., "A Rhetorical Theory of Diffusion," *Academy of Management Review* 29, no. 4 (2004): 653–69; James A. Herrick, *The History and Theory of Rhetoric: An Introduction*, 2nd ed. (Boston: Allyn and Bacon, 2001); William R. King and Jose L. Kugler, "The Impact of Rhetorical Strategies on Innovation Decisions: An Experimental Study," *Omega* 28, no. 5 (2000): 485–99; and Nitin Nohria and Brooke Harrington, "The Rhetoric of Change," research note no. 9-494-036 (Cambridge, MA: Harvard Business School, 1994); personal communication with Sandy Green.

44. Green, "A Rhetorical Theory of Diffusion," 659–60.

45. G. Thomas Goodnight and Sandy Green, "Rhetoric, Risk, and Markets: The Dot-Com Bubble," *Quarterly Journal of Speech* 96, no. 2 (2010): 115–40.

46. Green, "A Rhetorical Theory of Diffusion." See also Sandy E. Green, Marin Babb, and Can M. Alpaslan, "Institutional Field Dynamics and the Competition Between Institutional Logics: The Role of Rhetoric in the Evolving Control of the Modern Corporation," *Management Communication Quarterly* 15, no. 1 (2006): 7–16.

47. Green, "A Rhetorical Theory of Diffusion."

48. See, for example, Sandy Green and G. Thomas Goodnight, "Red

Queens and Black Swans: Argument Cascades and the Rational Evolution of Presumptive Risk Regimes During the U.S. Internet Bubble 1992–2002," paper presented at Academy of Management Meeting, Montreal, Canada, 2010.

49. See Can M. Alpaslan, Sandy Green, and Ian Mitroff, "Ethics, Rhetoric, and the Self as an Expanding Web of Conversations," *Current Topics in Management* 15 (2010); G. Thomas Goodnight and Sandy Green, "Work, Wealth, and Worry: The Benefits of Communication Study for Economic Literacy," *Communication Currents* 5, no. 6 (2010).

CHAPTER 9

1. Charles Perrow, *Normal Accidents: Living with High-Risk Technologies* (New York: Basic Books, 1984).

2. Ibid., 78.

3. Ibid., 96.

4. Perrow, *Normal Accidents*; see also Charles Perrow, "Organizing to Reduce the Vulnerabilities of Complexity," *Journal of Contingencies and Crisis Management* 7, no. 3 (1999): 150–55.

5. See, for example, Karlene H. Roberts, "New Challenges to Organizational Research: High Reliability Organizations," *Industrial Crisis Quarterly* 3 (1989): 111–25; Karlene H. Roberts, "Managing High Reliability Organizations," *California Management Review* 32, no. 4 (1990): 101–14; Karl E. Weick and Kathleen M. Sutcliffe, *Managing the Unexpected: Assuring High Performance in an Age of Complexity* (San Francisco: Jossey-Bass, 2001); and Erik Hollnagel, *Barriers and Accident Prevention* (Surrey, UK: Ashgate, 2004). For a systems-approach-based critique of "normal accidents" and "HROs," see Nancy Leveson, Nicolas Dulac, Karen Marais, and John Carroll, "Moving Beyond Normal Accidents and High Reliability Organizations: A Systems Approach to Safety in Complex Systems," *Organization Studies* 30, no. 2/3 (2009): 227–49. For a critique of the HRO theory, see Todd R. La Porte and Paula M. Consolini, "Working in Theory but Not in Practice: Theoretical Challenges in High Reliability Organizations," *Journal of Public Administration Research and Theory* 1 (1991): 19–47.

6. See, for example, Karlene H. Roberts, "Some Characteristics of One Type of High-Reliability Organization," *Organization Science* 1 (1990): 60–176; and Karlene H. Roberts, "New Challenges to Organizational

Research: High Reliability Organizations," *Industrial Crisis Quarterly* 3 (1989): 111–25.

7. Jeremy Siegel and Jeremy Schwartz, "Long-Term Returns on the Original S&P 500 Companies," *Financial Analysts Journal* 62, no. 1 (2006): 18–31.

8. Graciela Chichilnisky and Ho-Mou Wub, "General Equilibrium with Endogenous Uncertainty and Default," *Journal of Mathematical Economics* 42 (2006): 499–524.

9. Michel Callon, ed., *The Laws of the Markets*, Sociological Review Monographs (Malden, MA: Blackwell, 1998). See also Donald MacKenzie, Fabian Muniesa, and Lucia Siu (eds.), *Do Economists Make Markets? On the Performativity of Economics* (Princeton, NJ: Princeton University Press, 2007).

10. Donald MacKenzie and Yuval Millo, "Constructing a Market, Performing Theory: The Historical Sociology of a Financial Derivatives Exchange," *American Journal of Sociology* 109, no. 1 (2003): 107–45.

11. Robert H. Frank, Thoman Gilovich, and Dennis T. Regan, "Does Studying Economics Inhibit Cooperation?" *Journal of Economic Perspectives* 7, no. 2 (1993): 159–71. The authors argue that exposure to the self-interest model of economics makes individuals less cooperative. See also Robert H. Frank, *What Price the Moral High Ground? Ethical Dilemmas in Competitive Environments* (Princeton, NJ: Princeton University Press, 2004).

12. See, for example, Robert Olsen, "Trust, Complexity and the 1990s Market Bubble," *Journal of Behavioral Finance* 5, no. 4 (2004): 186.

13. Robert A. Haugen, *Beast on Wall Street: How Stock Volatility Devours Our Wealth* (Upper Saddle River, NJ: Prentice-Hall, 1999).

14. Ibid.

15. Ian I. Mitroff and Can M. Alpaslan, "Preparing for Evil," *Harvard Business Review* 81, no. 4 (2003): 109–15.

16. Khor H. Ee and Kee R. Xiong, "Asia: A Perspective on the Subprime Crisis," *Finance and Development* (June 2008): 19–23.

17. Harry Markopolos, *No One Would Listen: A True Financial Thriller* (Hoboken, NJ: Wiley, 2009).

18. Ian I. Mitroff, *Crisis Leadership: Planning for the Unthinkable* (Hoboken, NJ: Wiley, 2004). See also Karlene H. Roberts and Robert Bea, "Must Accidents Happen? Lessons from High-Reliability Organizations," *Academy of Management Executive* 15, no. 3 (2001).

19. MacKenzie and Millo, "Constructing a Market, Performing Theory."

20. Nassim N. Taleb, *The Black Swan: The Impact of the Highly Improbable* (New York: Random House, 2007).

21. Robert Shiller, *The Subprime Solution: How Today's Global Financial Crisis Happened, and What to Do About It* (Princeton, NJ: Princeton University Press, 2008).

22. Paul McCulley, "Teton Reflections," *Pimco*, August-September 2007, http://www.pimco.com/LeftNav/Featured+Market+Commentary /FF/2007/GCBF+August-+September+2007.htm (accessed September 20, 2007); and Bill Gross, "Beware Our Shadow Banking System," *Fortune*, November 28, 2007.

23. An internal assassination team (IAT) exercise is a special role-playing exercise Mitroff and his colleagues have used numerous times with executives. The technique helps executives suspend their moral or rational thinking and use their deep knowledge of the company's products, operations, and so on, to destroy the company. For instance, a medical insurance company used the technique to see that it was not equipped to detect certain types of scams that could force the company into bankruptcy. The company immediately formed counter-assassination teams to develop scam detection systems.

24. Shiller, *The Subprime Solution*.

25. Can M. Alpaslan, "Ethical Management of Crises: Shareholder Value Maximization or Stakeholder Loss Minimization," *Journal of Corporate Citizenship* (Winter 2009).

Note: Italic page numbers indicate figures and tables.